Psychology and 'Human Nature'

'I thought this an excellent book. I found the approach thought-provoking and innovative.'

Trevor Butt,
University of Huddersfield

'This is an extremely useful text which provides an insight into the debates surrounding human behaviour and the psychological models that inform our understanding.'

Ian Rivers,
College of Ripon & York St. John

Psychology and 'Human Nature' problematises what psychology usually takes for granted – the meaning of the psyche or 'human nature'. Peter Ashworth provides a coherent account of many of the major schools of thought in psychology and its related disciplines, including: sociobiology and evolutionary psychology, psychoanalysis, cognitive psychology, radical behaviourism, existentialism, discursive psychology and postmodernism. For each approach he considers the claims or assumptions being made about the psyche and their position on the associated issues of consciousness, the self, the body, other people and the physical world.

Psychology and 'Human Nature' will be essential reading for all students of psychology.

Peter Ashworth is Professor of Educational Research and Director of the Learning and Teaching Research Institute, Sheffield Hallam University.

Psychology Focus

Series editor: Perry Hinton, University of Luton

The Psychology Focus series provides students with a new focus on key topic areas in psychology. It supports students taking modules in psychology, whether for a psychology degree or a combined programme, and those renewing their qualification in a related discipline. Each short book:

- presents clear, in-depth coverage of a discrete area with many applied examples
- assumes no prior knowledge of psychology
- has been written by an experienced teacher
- has chapter summaries, annotated further reading and a glossary of key terms.

Also available in this series:

Friendship in Childhood and Adolescence
Phil Erwin

Gender and Social Psychology
Vivien Burr

Jobs, Technology and People
Nik Chmiel

Learning and Studying
James Hartley

Personality: A Cognitive Approach
Jo Brunas-Wagstaff

Intelligence and Abilities
Colin Cooper

Stress, Cognition and Health
Tony Cassidy

Types of Thinking
S. Ian Robertson

Psychobiology of Human Motivation
Hugh Wagner

Stereotypes, Cognition and Culture
Perry R. Hinton

Psychology and 'Human Nature'

▪ Peter Ashworth

First published 2000
by Psychology Press Ltd

27 Church Road, Hove,
East Sussex, BN3 2FA
http://www.psypress.co.uk

Simultaneously published in the
USA and Canada
by Taylor & Francis Inc
325 Chestnut Street, Suite 800,
Philadelphia, PA 19106

Psychology Press is part of the Taylor
& Francis Group

Typeset in Sabon and Futura
by Florence Production Ltd,
Stoodleigh, Devon

Printed and bound in Great Britain
by Biddles Ltd, www.biddles.co.uk

*British Library Cataloguing in
Publication Data*
A catalogue record for this book is
available from the British Library

*Library of Congress Cataloging in
Publication Data*
Ashworth, Peter D.
Psychology and 'human nature' /
Peter Ashworth
p. cm.
Includes bibliographical references
and index
ISBN 0-415-21299-5 (hbk)—ISBN
0-415-21300-2 (pbk).
1. Psychology. I. Title

BF121 .A77 2000
150—dc21

00-033761

ISBN 0–415–21299–5 (hbk)
ISBN 0–415–21300–2 (pbk)

Contents

Illustrations

Figures

Boxes

Series preface

The Psychology Focus series provides short, up-to-date accounts of key areas in psychology without assuming the reader's prior knowledge in the subject. Psychology is often a favoured subject area for study, since it is relevant to a wide range of disciplines such as Sociology, Education, Nursing and Business Studies. These relatively inexpensive but focused short texts combine sufficient detail for psychology specialists with sufficient clarity for non-specialists.

The series authors are academics experienced in undergraduate teaching as well as research. Each takes a topic within their area of psychological expertise and presents a short review, highlighting important themes and including both theory and research findings. Each aspect of the topic is clearly explained with supporting glossaries to elucidate technical terms.

The series has been conceived within the context of the increasing modularisation which has been developed in higher education over the last decade and fulfils the consequent need for clear, focused, topic-based course material. Instead of following one course of study, students on a modularisation programme are often able to choose modules from a wide range of disciplines to complement the modules they are required to study for a specific degree. It can no longer be assumed that students studying a particular module will necessarily have the same background knowledge (or lack of it!) in that subject. But they will need to familiarise themselves with a particular topic rapidly since a single module in a single topic may be only 15 weeks long, with assessments arising during that period. They may have to combine eight or more modules in a single year to obtain a degree at the end of their programme of study.

One possible problem with studying a range of separate modules is that the relevance of a particular topic or the relationship between topics may not always be apparent. In the Psychology Focus series, authors have drawn where possible on practical and applied examples to support the points being made so that readers can see the wider relevance of the topic under study. Also, the study of psychology is usually broken up into separate areas, such as social psychology, developmental psychology and cognitive psychology, to take three examples. Whilst the books in the Psychology Focus series will provide excellent coverage of certain key topics within these 'traditional' areas, the authors have not been constrained in their examples and explanations and may draw on material across the whole field of psychology to help explain the topic under study more fully.

Each text in the series provides the reader with a range of important material on a specific topic. They are suitably comprehensive and give a clear account of the important issues involved. The authors analyse and interpret the material as well as present an up-to-date and detailed review of key work. Recent references are provided along with suggested further reading to allow readers to investigate the topic in more depth. It is hoped, therefore, that after following the informative review of a key topic in a Psychology Focus text, readers not only will have a clear understanding of the issues in question but will be intrigued and challenged to investigate the topic further.

Introduction: psychology and 'human nature'

Introduction

THOUGH THIS IS NOT AN ABSOLUTELY UNCHALLENGED POSITION, contemporary academic psychology to a large extent views itself as a science. This seems to mean, certainly at undergraduate level, that it is not felt necessary for psychology to examine its most basic assumptions and presuppositions. Does physics, as taught, entail any reflection upon what is included or excluded in the scientific study of the material world? No – and neither is there any need in teaching psychology to raise the issue of what human nature might mean. In this book it is the meanings of 'human nature' that I wish to bring out. The scare quotes are to indicate that I see 'human nature' as a problem: the notion is not to be taken for granted.

The reader who is involved in the formal study of psychology, either as a specialism or as part of a degree whose centre of gravity lies elsewhere, will be able to use the book to locate the approach of the theories on which they are working within wider debates concerning human nature. Other readers, who are not formal students of the discipline but who may wish to increase the sophistication or range of their own thinking on human nature – the 'proper study' of us all according to the poet – will, I sincerely hope, equally find these pages of interest.

In this book, then, I consider several viewpoints on human nature, chosen for their diversity, contemporary impact, and relevance to the broad field of psychology. But it must be stressed that relevance to the field does not mean, necessarily, that a viewpoint lies *within* the field. Several theorists discussed here would firmly reject the label 'psychologist'. For instance, Sartre said in an interview conducted close to the end of his life, 'I do not believe in the existence of psychology. I have not done it and I do not believe it exists' (Schilpp, 1981: 28). Nevertheless the grounds for this statement relate to Sartre's understanding of the nature of human life, so – whatever academic discipline it falls within, if any – it is certainly relevant to 'psychology' as far as this volume is concerned. To reach a perspective on the discipline requires that we pay attention to those who would reject psychology. Among them are authors who, like Sartre, are antagonistic to the notion that there can be any stable meaning to 'human nature' at all, and reject psychology, thinking that psychologists are necessarily committed to such 'essentialism'. (Though some more recent views, such as those of the discursive psychologists represented in Chapter 6, indicate that this is too partial a view of the discipline as a whole.) The aim of all this is to help the reader see each viewpoint – some familiar, some new – in the context of a general problematic: What are the claims or assumptions which are being made about the subject matter, the human being?

The book is structured in a rough-and-ready way in terms of authors' explicit or implicit assumptions about whether 'human nature' should be regarded as ontologically primary or whether it is derivative of some more primordial reality. Ontology is concerned with the question of being. So what I mean by 'ontologically primary' is whether human nature is its own special kind of being or whether it is better understood through a more general or basic field of research. Of course, biology and culture are the prime candidates for primacy: many thinkers treat human nature as best studied in the wider context of biological or sociological research. Representatives of both these views appear in the following pages. But it is also of great interest that there are authors who do take neither the sociological path nor that of biological science but insist instead that personal 'psychological' life (they might not use the term 'psychological' for various reasons) is indeed ontologically primary. And this brings us to the profound question of whether, when we take psychological life to be its own special form of reality, this can still be treated as subject to scientific laws (such as the ones sought by cognitive psychologists) or whether some version of voluntarism, in which the person has individual freedom and responsibility, is necessary.

Of course, not all kinds of scholarly thought about the nature of the individual will be discussed here. Anglo-American philosophical thought is mostly not represented in this book. Nor is theological thinking covered. Religious thought does indeed deal with human nature but always as a secondary theme to the question of ultimate meaning. For a scholarly account of the treatment of human nature in a wide range of religions, east and west, see Ward (1998). Incidentally, he includes a discussion of what he calls 'evolutionary naturalism' in that book – for he regards the approach of Darwinists (to which I devote Chapter 1) as providing an interesting variation on certain religious themes regarding human nature.

Theological and certain philosophical approaches are left out, then, and sociology is only here at the 'micro' level, in which the human actor comes into focus. So there has been selection; but not arbitrary selection. In line with the structure I have outlined, the approaches discussed vary in the extent to which *social* or *biological* factors are emphasised as *determining* thought and action, or whether personal *freedom* is taken as characterising human nature, and voluntary decision-making is taken to be a real possibility.

Outline of the book

There is great scholarly merit in the unification of knowledge. It is an aim of science to draw disparate phenomena together under a coherent set of explanatory principles. So the possibility that the whole spectrum of psychological work may be grounded in mechanisms whose nature is fundamentally biological is very attractive, even if it is, at present, only an aspiration of some researchers and theorists. The two approaches dealt with in Chapters 1 and 2 are usually seen as rather distinct in the kind of psychology they generate, but they are united in at least this feature: both the ***evolutionary perspective*** and ***psychoanalysis*** suggest that human nature is fundamentally biological. They do so by claiming that this is because biology is the ultimate source of human motivation.

In the case of the evolutionary perspective, the ultimate motive is survival, in the sense that it is postulated that the process of evolution has selected psychological characteristics which serve to increase the likelihood of continuity over the generations. For psychoanalysis, on the other hand, the ultimate motive – equally unbeknown to the individual person – is sexual. In making the claim that there is an ultimate motive, both approaches face challenges of interpretation. How can an account of human nature which is built on such a narrow basis of biological motivation cover such a variety of both cultural and individual differences in actions and apparent motives?

In Chapter 1 I have selected homosexuality as the focus of a discussion of the approach of evolutionary theorists to a specific issue of human nature. Homosexuality is a special problem for the evolutionary perspective because it remains an enigma how a sexual orientation which obviously markedly reduces the individual's reproductive fitness nevertheless remains significant within the human gene-pool. But each subsequent theory also finds homosexuality enigmatic. So in each of the following chapters I have specifically discussed it – and it therefore provides a basis for the comparison of theories.

In Chapter 3 I turn to ***cognitive psychology***. For maybe the majority of research psychologists, cognitive psychology *is* psychology, or at least it is the scientific core of the discipline. Cognition is the process by which we attain knowledge. It includes perception, remembering, thinking, reasoning, imagining and learning. Psychology is understood by cognitive psychologists to be a biological science, and it is expected that, in the long run, the views psychologists progressively develop concerning mental processes will converge with the findings of neurologists and other biological scientists interested in brain function. Indeed, work at this interface, attempting to investigate research questions through a direct study of the brain, is of growing importance.

Yet in Chapter 4 we find in the influential work of B.F. Skinner a critique of cognitive psychology. Indeed, the theories of the whole of the rest of the book can be seen as agreeing in some way with this critique, however they might differ in other ways with Skinner's ***behaviourism***. Skinner wants to assert, primarily, that the human being is intrinsically engaged in the world. More than this, there is a sense in which the person is not separable from the world. I am simply the place where a number of variables interact, and so 'my' behaviour is not *mine* but the direct lawful outcome of those variables.

Now, though this book is not organised along historical lines, a reader may be forgiven a moment of puzzlement. Cognitive psychology largely arose in the context of a critique of behaviourism. Might it not therefore have been more rational to introduce behaviourism first, reversing the order of Chapters 3 and 4? After all, the two approaches to human nature are not very different in their positions on the two organising dimensions of the book; they both regard psychology ultimately as a biological science and they both adopt a deterministic stance. It does, however, seem to me that historical sequencing, in drawing out some connections necessarily downplays others (but see Richards, 1996, for a positive application of the historical perspective). My chosen ordering allows us to see that there is a surprising closeness between Skinnerian behaviourism and Sartrism.

In some ways Skinner's determinism is the extreme opposite of the ***existentialism*** of Sartre, which is the focus of Chapter 5. For in Sartre we have the outstanding example of a voluntarist – a position which I feel it is particularly important to represent in these pages precisely because the emphasis on freedom is so contrary to the scientific determinism assumed in psychology generally. Yet both Sartre and Skinner are anti-cognitivists. They deny with equal vehemence the idea of an 'inner life'. If in Skinner all 'choices' are really determined, and if in Sartre we are responsible for the significance we give even to 'determinants', nevertheless both place us firmly in the world. It is here that whatever human nature is must be found – not 'in our heads'.

The focus of Sartre and Skinner on the externality of 'mental' life is continued by the authors brought together in Chapter 6. The ***symbolic interactionists***, ***discourse analysts*** and ***discursive psychologists*** share a very radical social view of human nature. G.H. Mead, Erving Goffman and the rest share the vision of John Donne that 'no man is an island entire of itself'. The notion that mind and the self make up a firmly distinguishable inner world is illusory, for it is interaction with others within a shared culture conveyed by language and other systems of symbols which provides our possibilities of thought and identity. If we wish to know human nature, then, the approach must be through knowledge of the *discourses* within which we live and think.

It is not a great leap from this group of authors to those I discuss in the final chapter. ***Postmodern*** thought – hard to characterise – has, at least as one feature, an emphasis on discourse. In fact, this is carried to the point where we have a direct, deconstructive critique of the claim that there is any such thing as 'human nature'. This very idea may well be culturally specific so that other epochs or societies have no place within reality for the idea of a 'human nature'. The implication is, postmodernism asserts, that under such circumstances there is indeed no such thing as human nature. And so it is appropriate to have postmodernism as the final chapter of the book. But I have not allowed it to have quite the last word. In the Conclusion I briefly indicate certain features that I would personally wish to emphasise in a theory of human nature.

Criteria of comparison

It is in the Conclusion also that I mention some factors which I regard as essential to any understanding of human nature whatsoever. This is a strong assertion, and one which could be defended only in a different kind of book to this one (but see Merleau-Ponty, 1962; van den Berg, 1972). But my belief that it is so leads me to choose them as the basis for comparison and debate in looking at the wide range of views tackled in the book. So I have ended each chapter by summarising authors' positions on the *place in their understanding of human nature* of consciousness, the self, the body, other people, and the physical world.

- *Consciousness.* What place is given in the theory to the fact that human beings are aware? Plainly any author who takes the view that human freedom is real will give a central place to consciousness, whereas theorists who emphasise the determining role of society or biology may either downplay individual awareness or try to show that a particular personal outlook is the result of societal or biological processes and is not to be regarded as primary.

- *The self*. The importance of identity, selfhood, or the person's awareness of his or her own characteristics is a second key question to be put to each viewpoint. A thinker who adopts a biological stance will give a different weight to the self (possibly a lower one) than will a socially inclined author. This said, many social theorists regard selfhood as merely a product of the individual's place within the multifaceted structure of their society. Indeed, it is often argued that cultures vary in whether the self has much meaning at all in the face of the whole collectivity. A different line of argument is that, in coming to an awareness of self, we begin to have access to some degree of choice of what kind of person we wish to be.
- *The body*. Biological science can be expected to stress the body as the place where various causal factors interact and lead the person to act and think in the way they do. Yet there is a sociology of the body, and theories may very well stress the way in which social and historical circumstances come to dictate the person's view of their own body. Maybe, then, the body is best thought of as a social construction rather than that definite object which biological scientists claim to be describing.
- *Other people*. We will find that, at many points on the spectrum between biological science and social theory, authors try to express the inseparability of the individual and the collectivity. Biologists note that human evolution has always been in the context of an ecology which includes, as a major part, other people. So the individual's developing mental life 'presupposes' other people. Sociologists take the individual to be an intrinsic part of the culture, with the result that the person owes their 'individual psychology' to the influence of other members of the collectivity.

- *The physical world*. Perhaps less obvious than the earlier questions, but equally important, is the issue of how the person's relation to the physical world is theorised. I have mentioned that, for Skinner, the person has no distinct reality and must be viewed as just one element in the web of causes and effects which constitutes the objective world as a whole. At the other extreme, the 'objective world' is itself a human construction. In other cultures (or simply in other people's mental life, as a result of their biography) the world is a very different place.

In putting these five categories forward as ways in which views of human nature can be clarified I am, of course, seizing the right to provide an author's spin. But no book is spinless! I hope that one effect of the account of the varying meanings of 'human nature' laid out in these pages is to alert the reader to the most insidious spin of all. That is the pretence of recounting 'the facts' without any standpoint, perspective or position.

Chapter 1

The ultimate biological motive: the evolutionary perspective

chapter 1

CAN PRESENT-DAY HUMAN BEHAVIOUR be explained as the outcome of natural selection? A range of authors have argued that this is a fruitful way of viewing human nature. In this chapter I am going to treat sociobiology (Wilson, 1975, 1978), evolutionary psychology (Barkow *et al.*, 1992), and kindred viewpoints (e.g. Dawkins, 1976, 1982, 1989) together. However, it is right to register the fact that there are differences of emphasis between these accounts. Wilson's sociobiology puts forward an evolutionary explanation of certain characteristics of human social behaviour. The evolutionary psychologists do not seriously dissent from Wilson's analyses, but do insist that cognitive processes must be explicitly taken into account. For them, evolution is best seen as selecting particular tendencies of mental activity, which then appear in various guises in a wide range of human behaviour. They consider Wilson's concern with the evolution of social behaviour to neglect the evolution of the functions of the brain.

The other major way in which the authors discussed in this chapter differ is on the question of whether social behaviour is directly explicable in terms of biology and evolution, or whether culture has become somewhat independent of biology. Tooby and

Cosmides (1992), for instance, take the view that mental organisation has tendencies which are 'ingrained', and that it is only in conformity with these evolved characteristics that a particular form of culture or social behaviour can exist. Wilson takes this view, too, and writes:

> culture is ultimately a biological product. . . . It has been said that there are no genes for building airplanes. That of course is true. But people build airplanes to conduct the primitive operations of human beings, including war, tribal reunions, and bartering, which conform transparently to their biological heritage.
>
> (Wilson, 1996: 107)

In contrast, Dawkins insists that a quite different process from Darwinian evolution is involved in social behaviour. As we shall see, he believes that the elements of culture are propagated through human communication, and this accounts for the fact that they change far more rapidly than biological evolution allows. Dawkins has been castigated by other evolutionists for not showing orthodox Darwinian thinking in allowing such independence to social behaviour (see Dawkins, 1989: 193).

What the evolutionary perspective is trying to do

Human characteristics are an evolutionary product

Sociobiology and evolutionary psychology attempt to account for the behaviour of animals, including human beings, in terms of evolutionary adaptation to the environment. This means that there is a universal human nature based in evolved psychological mechanisms. Cultural variability exists, certainly, but this is taken as providing 'insight into the structure of the psychological mechanisms that generated it' (Barkow *et al.*, 1992: 5). Basic, universal human nature is the product of natural selection. Human characteristics are, in fact, 'adapted to the way of life of Pleistocene hunter-gatherers, and not necessarily to our modern circumstances' (ibid.). It is a basic assumption, then, that human psychological mechanisms have been selected by the evolutionary process because they were functionally adaptive. Note, however, that the main impact of evolution was during the millions of years of human prehistory.

Proximal motivations are explicable in terms of the ultimate motivation of (evolutionary/genetic) survival

Behaviour can be explained 'proximally' or 'ultimately'. Proximal explanations are couched in terms of immediately apparent motives – defence of territory, courtship, food searching, etc. Ultimate explanations give a more fundamental account of such proximal motives. The proximal motives are taken to be *expressions* of the basic motive, which is the one which relates the animal's behaviour to evolutionary advantage. So, if a particular pattern of courtship exists we can say that it has survival value. The ultimate explanation for the behaviour is simply that the behaviour was selected; that is, animals exhibiting it survived and reproduced.

Evolutionary theory

It is often stated that the major destructive impact of Darwin's evolutionary theory on traditional thinking was the idea that *homo sapiens* 'descended from the apes' (as it is put). Human beings are merely one biological species among the rest. The dominant and noble position of humans over the natural world is debunked; evolutionary theory removes human beings from the central place in the order of things. Important though this implication of Darwin may be, I am convinced that there is a much more significant thought in the theory, and one which is in some ways more disturbing of our understanding of the natural world and our place in it. That is, the idea of *purposelessness*. Evolution has no plan or intention.

Within the culture there still seems to be a residue of a certain medieval world-view in which the whole of creation is engaged in striving towards perfection. For instance, Eckhart (1260–1329), whose approach to religion is masterly, is nevertheless a bad source for an evolutionary understanding of the natural world: 'It is the nature of every grain of corn to become wheat and every precious metal to become gold and all procreation to lead to the procreation of the human race' (Eckhart, 1994: 113). This purposefulness is precisely the imagery that evolutionary theory opposes.

What happens is roughly as follows:

- Given that there is *variation* in characteristics between individual members of a species – whether it be in their physiology, anatomy or behaviour – and
- given that there are aspects of the *environment* – climate, resources for survival (food, places for nurturing young, etc.), other biological forms (including predators, parasites, competitors for resources, and so on), and members of the same species with whom to compete, mate or cooperate – for which some of the variants between individuals are more appropriate,
- then individuals who – by chance – have the more appropriate characteristics for the environment will be more likely to *survive*, reproduce, and have viable offspring who themselves survive to reproduce.
- The statistical effect of this process is an *unintentional* selection of those variants with the more appropriate characteristics, and the extinction of the forms 'less fitted' to the environment. This is 'descent with modification'.

Darwin's summary statement towards the end of *The Origin of Species* (first published, 1859) runs as follows

> That many and serious objections may be advanced against the theory of descent with modification, I do not deny. I have endeavoured to give them their full force. Nothing at

> first can appear more difficult to believe than that the more complex organs and instincts have been perfected . . . by the accumulation of innumerable slight variations, each good for the individual possessor. Nevertheless, this difficulty, though appearing to our imagination insuperably great, cannot be considered real if we admit the following propositions, namely, that all parts of the organisation and instincts offer, at least, individual differences – that there is a struggle for existence leading to the preservation of profitable deviations of structure or instinct – and, lastly, that gradations in the state of perfection of each organ may have existed, each good of its kind. The truth of these propositions cannot, I think, be disputed.
>
> (Darwin, [1859] 1994: 404)

'Nothing at first can appear more difficult to believe than that the more complex organs and instincts have been perfected . . . by the accumulation of innumerable slight variations, each good for the individual posessor'. Yet this is the Darwinian claim. There is no 'in order to . . .' in evolution, despite the lax talk of popular accounts. I want to stress again the need for very careful language in discussing the evolutionary perspective. Even the most distinguished writers engage in the dangerous metaphors of 'self-sacrificing ants' and 'intelligent genes' (Hamilton, 1972: 193, 195); 'selfish genes' and 'arms races' between parasite and victim (Dawkins, 1976, 1982: 55), and of the 'struggle among individual organisms to promote their own personal reproductive success' (Gould, 1997: 34). All these writers are explicit in acknowledging that the attribution of intelligence, selfishness, or struggle to genes or organisms is only a form of words, and that there is no purpose in what goes on. However, it is a (doubtless unintentional) betrayal of Darwin's project to downplay in any way the purposelessness and directionlessness of evolution.

Clarification 1: Distinguishing and rejecting Lamarckian evolution

Since Darwin's time the theory of evolution has been refined, so that the inheritance of *acquired characteristics* and the inheritance of *genetically* given characteristics have been sharply distinguished. The first of these, associated with Lamarck, is not currently accepted by biologists; the second is regarded as the basic process of evolution. Bodily features or mental skills which are developed in the course of life – strong muscles through exercise, speed in arithmetic through practice in book-keeping – would be instances of acquired characteristics, and these are not passed on to offspring. Inheritance has to pass through the filter of sexual reproduction, and if a characteristic is not represented in genetic material, it is not inherited.

The modern understanding of the process of evolution is that it occurs when, within the variation in the genetic constitution of members of a species, there is a characteristic which happens to be beneficial to survival. The advantageous characteristic will tend to be perpetuated since individuals who have it will be more likely to survive to breed and facilitate the survival of their offspring.

Clarification 2: The theory of inheritance

The major gap in Darwinian theory was the absence of any account of the process of inheritance. What was it that was actually transferred from parent to offspring, with variations on which natural selection would act? The theory of genetics, whose basic form was developed by Mendel, postulates discrete factors (genes) which carry information which guides embryo development. Each of the very large number of genes is one of a pair. Biological inheritance comes about from the fact that one gene of each pair is provided in the sex cells, or gametes, of each parent.

Clarification 3: The rejection of mutationism

If selection simply acts on naturally occurring variants in the genetic make-up of individuals, the immense range of species which has evolved seemed at first not to be explicable in terms of Darwinian evolution. Dobzhansky (1937) provided the first clear, detailed account of the evolutionary process expressed in genetic terms. Statistical modelling, with empirical support, showed that natural selection could, indeed, lead to the major evolutionary changes which are observed, without mutation having the central influence.

Clarification 4: DNA and the gene

Since 1953, with Watson and Crick's work on the structure of DNA (deoxyribonucleic acid), the application of molecular biology to the theory of evolution has been the most significant line of research. DNA is the hereditary material contained in the chromosomes of the nucleus of every cell. The effect of the genetic information contained in the DNA is open to investigation by correlating (a) variations in genes at a particular location on the chromosome (answering the question, What allele – version – of the gene do we have here?) with (b) the anatomical, physiological or behavioural characteristics of the organism (that is, the 'phenotype' generated by the gene).

'Genotype' refers to the genetic make-up of the individual; 'phenotype' refers to the expression of the genes in actual bodily structure or function or in psychological tendencies. Aspects of the environment – even the fact that a gene has an environment of other genes – enter into any phenotypical expression.

The unit on which evolution acts and the question of 'altruism'

The individual organism

Darwin certainly took the individual as the unit of selection. We may say that, for him, species evolve because individuals are differentially selected due to the relative adaptedness of their phenotypes to the environment. But a certain class of behaviour has been seen for many years as problematical for the view that it is on the individual organism that selection operates. The persistence of *altruistic* behaviour seems not to be explicable in this way.

How does altruism get established as characteristic, inherited behaviour of a species? After all, an altruistic individual may act in a self-sacrificial way in response to the perception that a fellow is under attack, in difficulties, or otherwise threatened. Altruism would put the individual animal in greater danger than would concern for self, and so the trait might be expected to quickly die out. For example, if there is genetic variation amongst bees in whether or not to sting an intruding bee which is not a member of the hive, alleles which promote such behaviour would lead to the death of the bee.

Human beings are regarded, within the evolutionary perspective, as sometimes behaving altruistically in a similar way. Wilson writes:

> Such an explanation immediately poses a basic problem: fallen heroes don't have any more children. According to the narrow mode of Darwinian natural selection, self-sacrifice results in fewer descendants, and the genes, or basic units of heredity, that allow heroes to be created can be expected to disappear gradually from the population.
>
> (Wilson, 1996: 80–81)

Individuals with alleles promoting less altruistic behaviour would surely rapidly out-reproduce altruists, and 'selfishness' would become characteristic of the species. But this does not happen. Why not?

The group

Wynne-Edwards (1962; see also Gould, 1977) put forward the view that groups are the units on which natural selection acts. Take, for instance, the regulation of reproduction in a certain species' population. Wynne-Edwards hypothesised that a group of members of the species might have a sensitivity to certain pressures of the environment year by year. That being so, they might restrain their breeding in years of scarcity. Plainly – and Wynne-Edwards recognised this – such behaviour would go against Darwin's focus on individual selection, since the individual would be behaving altruistically, refraining from personal reproduction 'for the good of the group'. The advantage to the group would be that their population becomes appropriate to the resources available. But the picture of evolution which Wynne-Edwards paints is one in which selection operates at the level of groups, not individuals.

Critics of Wynne-Edwards's view pointed out that some of his examples could be reinterpreted in terms of individual fitness. (For instance, it might be advantageous to the individual to restrict reproduction to times of plenty, since the invested effort would be more likely to give rise to offspring for whom there were sufficient resources.) But an alternative line of explanation put forward to cover difficult cases was Hamilton's notion of inclusive fitness.

The notion of 'inclusive fitness' and kin selection

Let us take it that evolution is the history of the survival or disappearance of genetic material *per se*. Thus, a behavioural tendency that was disadvantageous to the organism would tend to be eliminated from the species' gene-pool. But if this same characteristic was *advantageous* to other individuals (was, in this terminology, 'altruistic') then it would not disappear if this same tendency was represented in the individuals who survived – and whose survival was rendered more likely by the sacrifice.

Hamilton's (e.g. 1972) notion of inclusive fitness develops this account of altruism. Looked at in this light, the demise of a particular individual would not make a difference if the genetic material continued in existence. Fitness, which is synonymous with escaping evolutionary de-selection, is not just a matter of the individual, but of the effect of the individual's behaviour on the distribution of genes within the population. This is *inclusive fitness*.

The argument which draws on the notion of inclusive fitness is about how certain genetically determined behavioural characteristics, which seem very liable to suffer extinction – such as altruistic behaviours – actually do not disappear. So it is a model to explain why natural selection does *not* affect altruism in the way expected. In sum, the argument is that the more closely related the benefited are to the altruistic benefactor, the more likely it is that they also carry the gene for that altruism. Thus, altruism will be more likely to be preserved in the gene-pool if there is kinship between the altruist and those benefited.

Evolutionary geneticists do argue that, as a matter of general fact, altruism is more likely to be shown by one individual for another, the closer in kinship they are to the altruistic one. Hamilton (1972) developed a probabilistic argument, which shows the importance, in the 'decision' of whether to be selfish or altruistic, of relatedness. A sacrifice on behalf of two full siblings, where the altruistic individual dies without progeny but saves those siblings to reproduce, would be adaptive. The level of genetic relatedness between siblings is 0.5; on average brothers and sisters share half their genetic material. The gain as a result of the sacrifice is that two lives are saved. The calculation of advantage is $0.5 \times 2 = 1$. The altruistic act would not be adaptive were the relatedness to be less.

Now, as often expressed (and Hamilton expressed the situation in this way), we are led to think of the organism, or even the gene, as calculating the 'benefit to inclusive fitness' of an altruistic act. Sahlins (1977) is among those antagonistic to the evolutionary perspective who draw particular attention to the absurdity of the notion that organisms or even genes decide their actions on the basis of a calculation of inclusive fitness. It is as if, with Macbeth's witches, organisms are being accredited with the capacity to 'look into the seeds of time and say which grain will grow and which will not'. But this is not a correct view of the matter. Dawkins (1979) deals with the issue very clearly. No calculation of relatedness is implied by inclusive fitness; rather, kin selection is a way of explaining why certain behaviours which are disadvantageous to the individual nevertheless remain characteristic – in other words, why natural selection does *not* occur in these cases. It does not because other individuals who also have the characteristic are benefited. Under what conditions does an individual's sacrifice benefit other individuals whose genotype includes the altruistic gene? When the altruist and the benefited are kin. But this is not a calculation of the altruist – rather there is some mechanism for marking individuals who are to be benefited: maybe pheromones, perceptible familiarity (they are nest co-habitants, for example), and the organism has evolved the inclination to act altruistically towards such individuals, who will also tend to be kin.

It is also worth saying that the cost–benefit analyses which sociobiologists and others employ to make sense of animal and human behaviour also suffer from an inappropriately purposive language. For instance, consider the account of parenting differences between the sexes by Trivers (1971), which is generally accepted by evolutionists. He has it that females have a limited number of eggs, and they expend considerable energy and also suffer opportunity costs in the period of gestation. Therefore they may be said to have a greater investment in infants and thus are motivated to care for them. Males are correspondingly more motivated towards sexual activity, since this – rather than nurturing – will 'send their genes into the future'. Here we have *maximum expected utility* decision models. The payoff of a certain course of action can be calculated in terms of gene survival, and this should predict behaviour. Here again, the purposive imagery is misleading.

The gene or 'replicator'

So far it has been possible to take the view that natural selection operates on the individual organism. However, since what is inherited by offspring is supposed to be exclusively genetic material, it has been stressed famously by Dawkins (1976, 1982, 1989) that evolution operates on the genes rather than the individual. In line with this, Dawkins writes that Hamilton's notion of inclusive fitness was a last-ditch stand to retain the individual organism as the unit of selection. Inclusive fitness should really be regarded as tied to gene (or 'replicator') selection, says Dawkins:

> A replicator may be said to 'benefit' from anything that increases the number of its descendant ('germ line') copies. To the extent that active germ-line replicators benefit from the survival of the bodies in which they sit, we may expect to see adaptations that can be interpreted as for bodily survival. . . . To the extent that active germ-line replicators benefit from the survival of bodies *other* than those in which they sit, we may expect to see 'altruism', parental care, etc. To the extent that active germ-line replicators benefit from the survival of the group of individuals in which they sit . . . we may expect to see adaptations for the preservation of the group. But all these adaptations will exist, fundamentally, through differential replicator survival.
>
> (Dawkins, 1989: 84–85)

In criticism of this perspective, Gould (1977) points out that there is rarely a direct mapping of a gene onto a bodily structure. A number, often a huge one, of interacting genes is implicated. So 'when you amalgamate so many genes and tie them up in hierarchical chains of action mediated by environments, we call the resultant object a body' (ibid.: 24) and it is this that faces the hostile selection environment. This *is* an argument about selection (despite the denial of Dawkins, 1982: 116–117) in so far as the harsh selection environment of an organism does not select differentially for a certain allele but selects differentially between organisms in terms of their different configurations of physical and behavioural characteristics. The 'selfish gene' perspective, however appropriate it may be for some purposes, is not of interest to psychology nor does it have a bearing on the question of human nature. Nor does Dawkins (1989: 195–196) think it has such an application, unless 'the subject of our interest is natural selection' as such.

The problem of ultimate and proximal motives

We have seen that it is inappropriate to attribute 'evolutionary' purposiveness to replicators or organisms. The fundamental characteristic of natural selection is precisely its purposelessness. However, it is possible to speculate (and authors from the evolutionary perspective do enter into this speculation) that – without consciousness – people have tendencies of behaviour that reflect earlier adaptations. Gender roles are cited as an example.

The important thing to note here is that the idea of ultimate motive introduces a pervasive difficulty in the explanation of human behaviour. Simply, the question is how to account for the variety of human activity on the basis of such a narrow motivational theory. The challenge is to show that the ultimate biological motive of (inclusive) fitness is the explanation of the whole spectrum of proximal motives. In Box 1.1 I outline attempts by some evolutionists to account for homosexuality – which is a vexed issue indeed if this proximal motive is supposed to relate to the ultimate motive of evolutionary fitness. In forging the link between the range of actual human motives and the hypothetical ultimate motive we have what amounts to a particular type of hermeneutic problem; that is, a problem that is more akin to issues of *interpretation* than to matters of scientific cause. The task would seem to be to propose persuasive, coherent and illuminative narratives of the way in which such-and-such a piece of behaviour expresses (maybe indirectly) the ultimate motive. Writers from the evolutionary perspective have not developed skill in this form of psychological explanation. We will see in the case of Freudian theory how essential it is to construct such narratives if the link of many motives to one ultimate cause is to carry conviction at all.

Box 1.1 Homosexuality and the reproductive success of the species

The problem of homosexuality for evolutionary theorists is obvious. This proximal motivation would seem to be at odds with the ultimate motive of maximising evolutionary fitness. Symons has tried to account for homosexuality (using, it must be said, a very stereotyped image of gay and lesbian behaviour), arguing – in Alcock's condensed version:

> [T]he behaviour of male homosexuals, in Western society, is very different from that of female lesbians. Not only is male homosexuality much more common than the female variety, but males typically have a progression of partners, whereas their female counterparts have much more long-lasting, stable relationships. Symons's argument is that male homosexuals, although not necessarily advancing their genetic interests, are expressing the proximate mechanisms that motivate males to try to achieve sexual variety. The same mechanisms often drive heterosexual males to seek out multiple sexual partners and thereby increase their egg fertilisation opportunities.
>
> (Alcock, 1984: 523)

The separation of ultimate and proximate motivation is startling here, and there is no explanation of the basis of homosexual preference as such. In contrast, Wilson tries to account for the continuation over time of homosexuality. He argues, while confessing that the theory is speculative, that homosexuality is related to the ultimate motive as a mode of altruism:

> It is not inconceivable that in the early, hunter-gatherer period of human evolution, and perhaps even later, homosexuals regularly served as a partly sterile caste, enhancing the lives and reproductive success of their relatives by a more dedicated form of support than would have been possible if

they had produced children of their own. If such combinations of interrelated heterosexuals and homosexuals regularly left more descendants than similar groups of pure heterosexuals, the capacity for homosexual development would remain prominent in the population as a whole.

(Wilson, 1996: 83)

Dawkins (1982: 38) actually refuses to attempt a hypothetical link with the ultimate motive and indicates a hostility to explanations of the kind Wilson has put forward concerning homosexuality in Box 1.1. He argues that homosexuality is only a problem for the evolutionary perspective if there is a genetic component in the difference between homosexual and heterosexual individuals. Of course he is right, but this introduces the possibility of human motives that are not linked to the ultimate motive of maximising fitness. It is here that Dawkins does indeed break with sociobiologists and evolutionary psychologists, for he gives weight to a non-evolutionary, cultural process in the shaping of human behaviour, and introduces the idea that a 'unit of human knowledge' might be proposed for analytical purposes: the *meme*.

Memes: the quasi-evolution of culture?

Dawkins (1989) postulates the meme as a cultural replicator – 'a completely non-genetic kind of replicator, which flourishes only in the environment provided by complex, communicating brains':

> A meme should be regarded as a unit of information residing in the brain . . . It has a definite structure, realized in whatever physical medium the brain uses for storing information. . . . The phenotypic effects of a meme may be in the form of words, music, [etc.] . . . They may be perceived by the

> sense organs of other individuals, and they may so imprint themselves on the brains of receiving individuals that a copy (not necessarily exact) of the original meme is graven in the receiving brain. The new copy of the meme is then in a position to broadcast its phenotypic effects, with the result that further copies of itself may be made in yet other brains.
>
> (Dawkins, 1989: 109)

Dawkins supposes memes to be subject to a kind of evolutionary pressure. The 'fittest' ideas/fashions/artistic forms/religions/scientific theories survive. I think the analogy is supposed to be this: memes are to culture as genes are to the selection environment. The analogy breaks down very quickly. The product manager who thought that randomly occurring variants on the product, rather than carefully developed new designs, could be launched onto the market (a hostile selection environment), and evolutionary pressure would do the rest, would be out of a job. 'Memes' are often designed, thought out, not randomly generated. Their fate in the world – though not entirely rational – is due to their human meaning, not some kind of battle for reproductive advantage.

According to Dawkins himself (1982: 111–112), there are fundamental differences between meme and gene selection processes. In particular, there is no specifiable set of variants for memes as there is for a gene (a given gene is one of a set of alleles). There is a much more imprecise 'copying process' for cultural elements, whereas the production of gametes is a lawful biological process. Memes blend and interact with each other whereas genes remain discrete entities. And Lamarckian effects may occur.

> These differences may prove sufficient to render the analogy with genetic natural selection worthless or even positively misleading. My own feeling is that its main value may lie not so much in helping us understand human culture as in sharpening our perception of genetic natural selection.
>
> (Dawkins, 1982: 112)

Chapter 6 of this book is relevant to the debate. It is arguable that to view human 'information' in the way suggested by the notion of the 'meme' is so insensitive to the nature of communication, of meaning and of discourse, as to be invalidated as even a partial model of knowledge and its transmission/transformation.

Criticisms

The emphasis on ***biology as the major determinant*** of human social behaviour is said to culpably neglect culture and the structure of society. In response, Gould (1997) points out that the evolutionary perspective usually stresses aspects of human behaviour which it takes to be ***universal***. Cultural diversity is supposed to occur within parameters which are of evolutionary origin. Nevertheless, it is difficult to specify precisely what it is that is universal. Play is mentioned in Barkow *et al.* (1992), as is an aesthetic preference for certain landscapes over others. In discussion of presumed universals, ***careless analogies*** are sometimes drawn between human action and animal behaviour. For example, the account of altruism in evolutionary genetics is very different from the classic religious account, though the implication is that the evolutionary account is explanatory. The best-known text on altruism is Luke 10:25–37 'The Good Samaritan', the point of which is to extend friendship universally. Any limitation of altruism to one's own kin group or even national group is quite explicitly rejected.

The evolutionary perspective suggests that some of the characteristics which appear to differentiate between people are ***natural kinds***, attributable to evolution. Take the category *sexual orientation* for instance. We are encouraged to think that there are a limited set of evolutionarily determined types of people, each type having a certain sexual orientation. But what is this set? It seems as if the categories of sexual orientation recognised vary from society to society and from epoch to epoch. And what characteristics does the notion *sexual orientation* specify? Harré (1991) wonders whether it includes the division of domestic labour.

If not, what *is* evolutionarily specified? Harré doubts whether many of the characteristics which differentiate, for instance, male/female in current western society can be regarded as attributes of natural kinds of human being.

In discussing the variety of human motives, the ***distinction between proximal motives and the ultimate motive*** gives rise to problems of explanation. Though Sahlins's argument that no one consciously acts in order to maximise their inclusive fitness forgets the distinction between proximal and ultimate motivation, the link in human beings between the ultimate explanation of action and the plethora of motives for different behaviours is hypothetical – evidence is lacking.

Forms of human behaviour (e.g. birth control; fostering and adoption of unrelated infants, and homosexuality) which are hard to account for in terms of inclusive fitness, parental investment, etc., are ***explained in* ad hoc *ways***. Dawkins counters this objection in two ways (a) arguing that the evolutionary conditions which gave rise to human behaviour no longer apply and so one need not expect contemporary adaptedness, and (b) – more controversial among evolutionists – a distinction is possible between cultural and evolutionary determinants of behaviour.

Gould (1997) objects to the way in which ***evolutionary adaptation*** is used as an explanation, for modern behaviour is likely to be *lacking* in optimal adaptation. The Pleistocene conditions in which it evolved no longer apply. But then the task of those who wish to explain human behaviour in evolutionary terms becomes very problematical, since it depends on a speculative account of life in hunter-gatherer times.

Beyond purely theoretical or scientific considerations, the evolutionary perspective does seem to give ideological comfort to a form of ***conservative thought*** that denies the efficacy of social change in affecting basic human motives and behaviour. Barash (1979) is an example of this thinking. There is a marked tendency to racism, sexism, and caste/class elitism.

Summary

What view of human nature do the sociobiologists seem to be putting forward? Plainly, for them understanding of the broad parameters of human nature is to be sought by considering the evolutionary pressures from which the species emerged in the Pleistocene age. But, as I mentioned in the Introduction, in order to assist the reader to compare this view with others represented in subsequent pages I want now to indicate the line the theorists seem to be taking of the place in human nature of consciousness, the body, selfhood, others, and the physical world.

- *Consciousness*. Presumably, this feature of human beings and (diminishingly) of lower orders of life, has survival value. Certainly, conscious perception of the environment could be taken to be of evolutionary advantage. A certain level of thought must also have value. But whether, for instance, developed reflection has advantage is debatable.
- *Selfhood*. Like consciousness, my awareness of my personal being, my attribution of characteristics to this being, and my emotional investment in it, is a peripheral feature of humans. Hypothetically, it has emerged in the service of the survival of the genetic material. The idea of free action, clearly part of the meaning of human selfhood, is regarded as false.

> [I]f our genes are inherited and our environment is a train of physical events set in motion before we were born, how can there be a truly independent agent within the brain? The agent itself is created by the interaction of the genes and the environment. It would appear that our freedom is only a self-delusion.
>
> (Wilson, 1978: 71)

- *The body*. This is partly an expression of genetic inheritance, and is the 'carrier' of the genetic material through time. The genetic material is essential, the body is its ephemeral 'residence'. The body will pass the information of the genes on to subsequent generations, and this constitutes its – unconscious and non-purposive – 'task'.

- *Others*. Given the notion of inclusive fitness, the evolutionary perspective lends emphasis to the idea of kinship. It is said that, in the process of the evolution of the species, the demise of an individual, if it ensured the survival of sufficient kin, would be 'rational'. (The death of my self is of no interest in evolutionary terms.) However, it is to be noted that this does not imply intention, or a calculation of whether to be altruistic or not, on the part of the individual.

  Authors who take the evolutionary perspective are divided in their attitude to culture – it is either significantly moulded by evolution or may develop by an independent non-Darwinian process.
- *The physical world*. It is a selection environment. The physical world should be seen as an ecology in which the biological form is exposed to threats and aids to survival. It is where competition takes place, then, and where conditions obtain to which the expression of the individual's genetic material is well-adapted or maladapted. Since it seems agreed that human adaptiveness is to the way of life of Pleistocene hunter-gatherers, there is expected to be a certain friction between modern urban life and our genetic tendencies.

Further reading

Barkow, J. H., Cosmides, L. and Tooby, J. (1992) *The Adapted Mind: Evolutionary Psychology and the Generation of Culture*, New York: Oxford University Press. This is the major account of evolutionary psychology. The first chapter, 'The psychological foundations of culture' (pp. 19–136) by Tooby and Cosmides, provides an extensive theoretical overview. Most of the rest of the book deals with particular items of human behaviour which are thought explicable in evolutionary terms.

For background, the following deserve attention, starting, of course, with Darwin:

Darwin, Charles ([1859] 1994) *The Origin of Species by Means of Natural Selection*, London: Senate.

Wilson, E.O. (1978) *On Human Nature*, Cambridge, Mass.: Harvard University Press.

Dawkins, R. (1989) *The Selfish Gene* (2nd edn), Oxford: Oxford University Press.

Chapter 2

Mental conflict: biological drives and social reality

chapter 2

LIKE DARWIN, SIGMUND FREUD (1856–1939) is a towering figure in his impact on the direction of discussion concerning human nature. It could also be said that he invented the psychological approach to individual therapy which, like a kind of lay confessional, moves through verbal accounts of experience to seek understanding.

The attempt to grasp psychoanalysis as a contemporary movement is indeed best approached by going back to Freud. This is not just because of his foundership, nor just because of the lucidity of his writing, but because a clear view of the original stance of psychoanalysis is necessary as a basis for making sense of his contemporary legacy, which includes the plethora of psychotherapies. In some way they all owe their existence to Freud even if this arises from their rejection of one or other psychoanalytic tenet or practice.

So this chapter does not attempt to carry out a history of the psychoanalytic movement to the present. The focus is solely on Freud. But even with this restriction the task is a difficult one. I have not traced the important changes of substance or emphasis which he himself introduced, but have presented the theory ahistorically. So the question concerning the rejection of the 'seduction theory' in favour of the view that female reports of early abuse are phantasies is omitted (though it is a very weighty matter, given the dawning awareness today of the extent of childhood sexual abuse). Also omitted is the theoretically important introduction, late in Freud's work, of a 'death instinct' as a significant dynamic in mental functioning to complement the pleasure principle and reality.

What Freud was trying to do

Freud's principal work can be thought of as entailing three interrelated elements:

- a theory of neurosis
- a theory of normal psychological development
- a therapeutic technique

I regard the last of these as most significant: Freud's major achievement was the development of psychoanalysis as the means of understanding the individual in the therapeutic situation. Thus, the correct approach to the theory must be through a consideration of its interpretative role. Broadly, then, I am going to take it that *theory is in the service of the therapeutic technique*. It is in the psychoanalytic situation that, it is claimed, the theory is both tested and developed. Interestingly, Ricoeur (1998: 24) has recently confessed that his monumental work on Freud (Ricoeur, 1970) would have benefited from giving more serious attention to the process of therapy; he devoted exclusive attention to the theoretical writings.

Psychological causality and the development of mind

Freud's aim was to uncover the motives, not necessarily conscious ones, underlying mental life. All actions have a cause, even 'accidents'. Committed to science, as this was understood in his time, Freud's way of avoiding the dualism of mind and matter was to postulate a mental energy comparable to energy in the physical sciences. Libido, a basic sexual-aggressive energy, fulfils the role of grounding mental life in biological drives.

Freud aimed, then, to build a scientific, causal model of how libido gets channelled and transformed so as to power the whole range of human desires. This aspect of the theory is termed by Ricoeur (1970) 'energetics'. In his account of childhood he aimed to show how the undifferentiated, libidually motivated infant becomes a mentally complex and socialised adult.

Interpretation of unconscious meaning

Freud's work (in therapy and in the discovery of psychological facts generally) consisted of the attempt to interpret talk and behaviour in order to reveal the underlying desires. This aspect of Freud's work, in which he is proposing a theory of interpretation, a *hermeneutic* theory, is firmly distinguished by Ricoeur (1970) from energetics, the causal model of the mind.

It must be made clear that Ricoeur himself did not regard the apparently hard-to-reconcile dimensions of Freud's theory (the causal model of energetics and the hermeneutical theory) a defect. For him, the idea that human psychology is to be understood as biologically based, yet requiring a meaning-interpretation of its actual manifestations, is a strength. We shall see later (Chapter 6) that Ricoeur goes against many other writers on hermeneutics by saying that 'the text' – here, the material requiring interpretation – refers to non-textual (in Freud, biological) material. Indeed, this is the basis of the acrimony between Ricoeur and the French psychoanalyst Lacan (see Ricoeur, 1998: 68–70).

Dream interpretation: causality and hermeneutics

Freud himself regarded *The Interpretation of Dreams* (1976) as his major work. The original was actually published in 1899, but dated 1900 to indicate its place in the unfolding future of thought.

> It contains, even according to my present-day judgement [he is writing more than thirty years after the book's first appearance], the most valuable of all the discoveries it has been my good fortune to make. Insight such as this falls to one's lot but once in a lifetime.
>
> (Preface to English edition of 1932)

In it, as I have indicated, a valiant attempt is made to reconcile the two methodological tendencies of his work, *energetics* and *hermeneutics* (Ricoeur, 1970). One aspect of his approach to the understanding of dreams and mental life generally is steadfastly deterministic. All mental activity is the outcome of the channelling of libido, which Freud regarded as an energy of the same status as the recognised forms of energy of the physical sciences. But the second aspect of his approach to dreams is quite different. The *interpretation* of dreams is exactly that: what Freud was most centrally trying to do here was to provide a hermeneutic theory – a theory to guide interpretation. The interpretation of dreams is a matter of the analyst hearing the apparently unfathomable manifest dream content, and translating it back into a much more understandable set of latent dream thoughts.

> Every attempt that has hitherto been made to solve the problem of dreams has dealt directly with their *manifest* content as it is presented in our memory. . . . We are alone in taking something else into account . . . namely their *latent* content . . . We are thus presented with a new task which had no previous existence: the task, that is, of investigating the relations between the manifest content of dreams and the latent dream-thoughts, and of tracing out the processes by which the latter have been changed into the former.
>
> The dream-thoughts and the dream-content are presented to us like two versions of the same subject-matter in two different languages. Or, more properly, the dream-content seems like a transcript of the dream-thoughts into another mode of expression, whose characters and syntactic laws it is our business to discover by comparing the original and the translation.
>
> (Freud, 1976: 381; original emphasis)

Dreams are the expression of wishes. Yet the wishes tend to contravene prohibitions which are based in reality. So dreams involve compromise between desire and reality. Though reality is in part suspended in sleep, censorship is nevertheless active and the distortion of desire due to the censorship of the dreamwork is what has to be undone in interpretation.

Dreams, incoherent and illogical as they are, can be translated by attending to four basic processes:

- *Condensation.* There is no one-to-one mapping between manifest content and the underlying dream-thoughts. Manifest content is the outcome of a multiplicity of influences in which desires are woven in with elements derived from the residues of the day's activity.
- *Displacement.* It cannot be assumed that the most salient features of the manifest content reflect the most important motives of the latent dream-thoughts. Rather, the most emotionally charged aspects may appear as 'asides'. Additionally, an element in a dream may be replaced by a substitute, which has some association with the 'real' referent.
- *Representation.* Interpretation demands that visual imagery must be traced back to the dream-thoughts from which they arose; that is, by finding their verbal associations using free association.
- *Secondary revision.* In recalling, and certainly in intelligibly recounting a dream, there is a need for the dreamer to give some coherence to its 'events'. Interpretation entails breaking down this purely narrative coherence in order to retrieve the various meanings of the latent dream-thoughts.

The activity of the mind in 'disguising' the latent dream-thoughts so as to give rise to the manifest content is not an activity of consciousness. Indeed, Freud (1976: 751) concluded that '*the most complicated achievements of thought are possible without the assistance of consciousness*'.

Freud emphasised that the model of the structure of the mind found useful in understanding the process of dreaming is of general applicability. The dreamwork is not a special, isolated process. The unconscious, consciousness, and a censor which acts between 'form part of the normal structure of our mental instrument, and dreams show us one of the paths leading to the understanding of its structure' (Freud, 1986: 768–769). In an enthusiastic comment added to the 1909 edition of the book, Freud wrote, with emphasis: '*The interpretation of dreams is the royal road to a knowledge of the unconscious activities of the mind*' (Freud, 1976: 769).

Energetics and hermeneutics in the dream theory

In interpretation, the psychoanalyst is not simply tracing the path of a causal process – undoing the dreamwork to reveal the dream-thoughts – but, 'The dream-thoughts and the dream-content are presented to us like two versions of the same subject-matter in two different languages', and, furthermore, the meanings may be quite idiosyncratic. The psychoanalyst has to try to discover the language, by asking the analysand (the person being analysed) for free associations, as well as by drawing on wide-ranging knowledge of the world of the analysand, and employing imagination and empathy. This interpretative activity is far from the apparently mechanistic energetics. It is indeed a hermeneutic activity. Moreover, it is a particular mode of hermeneutics – and one which typifies psychoanalysis generally.

As Palmer (1969) points out, hermeneutics, originally used to refer to the rules governing the interpretation of sacred or classical texts, has in the last century been applied with very great generality to the process of coming to an understanding:

> something foreign, strange, separated in time, or experience, is made familiar, present, comprehensible; something requiring representation, explanation or translation is somehow 'brought to understanding' – is 'interpreted'.
>
> (Palmer, 1969: 14)

Ricoeur (1970) distinguished two extreme forms of hermeneutics. The *hermeneutics of meaning-recollection* aims at an interpretation of the full meaning of the thing being analysed. For example, it would be in accord with the hermeneutics of meaning-recollection for a psychological research methodology to involve interviewing research participants on some aspect of their experience; analysing the interview transcripts in such a way as to elicit their experience exceedingly faithfully, and then checking with the participants themselves after the analysis is done to ensure that the research account is faithful to their meaning. The *hermeneutics of suspicion* finds that – behind the thing being analysed – there is a further reality which allows a much deeper interpretation to be made and which can challenge the surface account. This is a critical analysis, carried out in a mode of suspicion, and looking beyond the conscious grasp which the person has. Of course, for Ricoeur, Freudian analysis was a clear instance of this form of critical thinking – behind actions, dreams and thoughts lay the more fundamental world of the unconscious, with its covert motives. We find the hermeneutics of suspicion fully developed in psychoanalytic practice.

Psychoanalytic practice

Since I have taken Freudian theory concerning the mind and its development to be, for the most part, in the service of therapy I must now indicate the nature of analytical therapy, following it with a gloss (as I confess, an ahistorical gloss) on the theory.

Roles in analysis

The person being analysed, confronted with the strange therapeutic situation in which all they are asked to do is to express their thoughts without reserve, will surely only have their own personal tendencies on which to base their perceptions. Such perceptions are *projections*, and as such constitute useful material for the analyst, since they reflect the personality of the patient.

The analyst will not simply fit in with the assumptions and desires of the analysand. This would not further the project of bringing their unconscious sources of motivation to light. For instance, behaving as an authoritative 'God Almighty' would merely reinforce the dependence or antagonism of the patient – whereas the aim would be to reveal it by challenging it.

> Freud . . . noted long ago that one should never underestimate the human being's irresolution and craving for authority. One of the analyst's temptations, much played on by the irresolute analysand, is to purvey wisdom when it would be more appropriate to the job at hand to analyse wisely.
>
> (Schafer, 1983: 11)

Ideally, the analyst will, among other things:

- provide safety, giving a 'holding environment', in which the analysand is free to express any and all thoughts and feelings;
- express no views about the goodness or badness of the analysand's behaviour or thoughts or feelings;
- show dispassionate concern – not using the relationship to satisfy their own needs, or imposing their own personality or preferences;
- be emotionally undemanding.

The relationship in therapy

The relationship between analysand and analyst is a prime source of material for analysis, and the dynamics have the constituents of transference and counter-transference, resistance and counter-resistance. In *transference*, the way the analysand has come to perceive people (from infancy onwards) is shown in his or her reaction to the analyst. See Box 2.1.

Counter-transference acknowledges the fact that the analyst will similarly project characteristics onto the patient. The analyst must notice this happening in order to stop the counter-transference affecting the relationship adversely, and to use the projection to further understand the patient (e.g. 'If I am reacting to the patient as if he were a dependent son, perhaps this is being forced on me because he is viewing me as a father figure').

Resistance is pervasive in psychoanalytic therapy according to Freud:

Box 2.1 Schafer on 'transference'

> A young man in analysis had been realizing in an ever more agitated fashion how disturbed and confined he had always felt in connection with certain characteristic features of his father's conduct. His father followed the strict policy of always behaving sensibly, responsibly, gently, and kindly; the man thus fit the familiar pattern of reaction formation against . . . sadistic modes of action. These were cruel in their effects, for they stimulated the son to think himself especially unworthy and unable to love . . . But the boy himself became more and more disposed to act sadistically, especially in the wishful fantasies he unconsciously elaborated.
>
> [One reason for this development] was that he angrily regarded his father as castrating in several ways: for one thing, he saw his 'blameless' father as setting a standard of controlled manhood he could never hope to meet . . . understandably, he had presented himself for analysis as a dispirited, cynical, indecisive, apathetic, melancholy person. Consciously [however], he professed only love and esteem for his father . . .
>
> (Schafer, 1983: 117–118)

At this point, Schafer draws attention to two significant points to bear in mind when reading the description of this case. Firstly, one does not know, and is not centrally interested in, whether the 'father' bears much relationship to the actual person, viewed 'objectively'. The issue is to unravel the son's 'father imago'. Secondly, the unravelling of this father imago was achieved through very careful analysis of the analysand's **transference***.*

> Returning now to the young man: one day when he was well into the analysis, he experienced one of his most anguished yet liberated and liberating moments during the analysis. He was recounting once again, but more insight-

fully than ever before, a scene that had been serving as a prototype of his childhood relation with his father. In the scene, his father had forbidden him to do something because it would have upset his mother. Thereupon the boy had stormed off to his room. His father had followed him and taken a long time, patiently and calmly, to explain and to justify his having issued the prohibition. It seemed that the father had determined, for his own neurotic reasons, to get his young son to agree that issuing the prohibition had been the right, kind, rational thing for him to have done.

(ibid.: 119)

In his analysis, the young man . . . had, among other things, been construing my consistently trying to understand him neutrally and impartially as a replication of his father's guilt-inducing and castrating actions, and he had been dealing with my interventions accordingly. That is to say, either he had been attacking me scornfully and vituperatively . . . or he had been acting despondently, ruminatively and inertly, sometimes concealing the latter by forcing himself to act jovially and zestfully, as he had been doing for his father.

(ibid.: 121)

> The resistance accompanies the treatment step-by-step. Every single association, every act of the person under treatment must reckon with the resistance and represents a compromise between the forces that are striving towards recovery and the opposing ones.
>
> (Freud, 1912: 103)

For various reasons – most importantly because people's irrational defences (though harmful) are defending them against what they take to be real threats – the analysand resists the analysis. Such resistance also requires interpretation. Resistance is a clinical concept that refers to the myriad of methods analysands use to obstruct the very process that they are relying on to help them.

Counter-resistance is the process in which the analyst fails to maintain a proper part in the analytical relationship. But again understanding can be assisted by reflection on counter-resistance.

Interpretation

Interpretation is of transference and resistance, of dreams, of reported behaviour, attitudes, thoughts and feelings; of defences, 'personal characteristics', etc., and providing a possible account of the reasons for these. The claim made earlier that psychoanalytic theory about the mind and about the development of the personality is best viewed as being in the service of therapy, and has the function of aiding the analyst in their interpretation, may become clearer here. The analyst will use theoretical formulations to make sense of the analysand's thoughts, feelings and behaviour, and some appropriate version of this interpretation will provide a new understanding for the analysand – one which will, ideally, enable her or him to act more freely in future.

Schafer (1983) treats the process as the co-authoring of a satisfactory account, which would *not* be how Freud would have discussed interpretation. For him, interpretation was the provision of scientific discoveries about the mental life of the analysand. Take, for example, the case of paranoia (Freud, 1979) which the sufferer, Schreber, himself documented (though not as a confession of delusion, but with a serious intent to persuade readers that certain opinions of his were true). This written account Freud analysed.

Schreber's delusions included the feeling that he was being persecuted: firstly by his former physician, Flechsig – whom he called a 'soul murderer' (Freud, 1979: 143) – and later by God. Freud argues minutely to the conclusion that the emotionality, which Schreber experiences, is unconsciously motivated by early relationships within the family. The earlier focus on the physician is initially interpreted tentatively: 'The patient was reminded of his brother or father by the figure of the doctor, he rediscovered them in him' (Freud, 1979: 182).

The move in focus to God is seen as an explicable escalation. Among other phantasies, there are ones in which Flechsig and God are both believed to be similarly 'disintegrated' into separate personalities. This leads to the conclusion that the figures carry equivalent meanings.

> All of this dividing up of Flechsig and God into a number of persons thus had the same meaning as the splitting of the persecutor into Flechsig and God. They were all duplications of one and the same important relationship.
>
> (Freud, 1979: 185)

Schreber's phantasies include the persistent experience of being under a form of physical attack by God (in which, however, Schreber is victorious), and the desire, which also seemed to be a divine requirement, that Schreber become a woman. Importantly, Schreber shows a mixture of reverence and rebelliousness to God. Such features of the case as this, together with the circumstance that Schreber's father had been an eminent doctor, lead Freud to the interpretation that God stands for Schreber's father and that the basis of the paranoia lay in the castration complex.

My claim that psychoanalytic theory is in the service of interpretation is seen in the relationship between theory and practice in the Schreber case. Freud makes it seem inevitable that the case is to be understood in terms of Schreber's early relationship to his father and in this way finds the facts in support of the theory of mental development. At the same time the notion of 'castration complex', which has been introduced, is a key component of that theory, and it is to the theory that we now turn.

Some basic ideas of psychoanalytic theory

Freud's theory is, through and through, a *conflict* theory rather than a *deficit* theory. It is not that some people are disadvantaged in their adjustment to the world by the lack of some skill or capacity; rather, he sees them as riven with mental struggle. The key features of Freud's theorising of the struggle are its unconscious nature; its basis in a biological drive, libido, and the incompatibility between libidinal desire and the requirements placed on the individual by society.

The concept of the *unconscious* is plainly foundational for Freud. We have seen in the dream theory that he stressed the view that mental life is by no means confined to conscious activity. In fact, unconscious activity is primary; the true psychological reality in the sense that it is *this* which must be understood in order to understand the person. Conscious experience is a compromise, defensively constructed as a result of the contrary pressures of inner desire and outer necessity.

Desire is an energy, *libido*, and ideas – that is, all mental contents – are energised (cathected) to a greater or lesser extent. They are emotionally charged. From the start sexuality is a principle motive of human behaviour. As a drive, libido is of great urgency in demanding gratification. However, it is exceedingly malleable in the ways in which it may be expressed. It is also prone to a wide variety of modes of development.

The conflict between *desire and necessity* is to be seen as the general form which mental strife takes. Life with other people requires a constant renunciation of desire (the 'pleasure principle') in the face of external reality or 'necessity'. This entails a redirection of libido. Mental conflict is largely to be understood as an internal, unconscious dynamic entailing the repression of socially disapproved expressions of the pleasure principle. These are substituted by behaviour and thoughts which, though acceptable, have the function of 'discharging' libido associated with the repressed.

Another way of viewing this process is that the individual has been socialised. Appropriate behaviour has been learned, which is 'energised' and made valuable to the individual by the fact that it draws on the charge of libido linked with the unacceptable behaviour that is now repressed. Behaviour associated with the 'reality principle' is therefore powered, so to speak, by the fact that it unconsciously represents quite unacceptable behaviour associated with the 'pleasure principle'.

The 'topographies'

The 'first topography', or mental map, is the structure already mentioned that we found essential to *The Interpretation of Dreams*. The 'second topography', which Freud introduced in 'The ego and the id' (1923; see Freud, 1984) gives us a tripartite model of the mind:

- *Id* is the aspect of mental life which consists of desires and drives, and is governed by the 'pleasure principle'. Biological in its origin, it is this function of the mind to which I refer in the title of the chapter. Yet over time the purely biological content of the id is overlain with repressed material of all kinds.
- *Ego* is that aspect of mental life which is directed towards reality. It accomplishes the compromise between desire and necessity, and is governed by the 'reality principle'. Note that ego derives from id – all mental life is energised by libido. Since reality prevents the direct realisation of many desires, awareness of reality is needed to allow at least some desires to be realised in at least some form. Aspects of the ego (such as the mechanisms of ego defence – see below) are unconscious.
- *Superego* is the internalised awareness of the norms and values of society (via the socialising influence of the family). Ego has to take this into account, also, in deciding a course of action that is a compromise between desire and necessity. Superego is also far from totally conscious. Its punishing force, felt as guilt, borrows libido energy.

The introduction of the second topography shows a feature rather typical of the development of psychoanalytical theory. It is noticeable that the id/ego/superego formulation does not supplant the first topography; it is not an improvement on it, and the first topography remains indispensable. The two models of the mind do not easily fit together, yet both are true. What we have is a gradual historical accretion of descriptive models and terms, which relate only roughly to each other.

The conflict between desire and necessity gives rise to a lot of 'energetic' phenomena – things that have to do with the distribution of mental energy, such as the repression of desires which conflict with reality, rendering them unconscious. Such desires remain energised, and 'strive' for expression. They may emerge in disguised, symbolic, and neurotic forms. Repression is a defence mechanism.

Mechanisms of ego defence involve the distortion of perception so as to avoid the tension of the conflict between desire and necessity. Other examples are:

- Denial – of a fact of reality or a desire or instinct
- Projection – of personal characteristics to others (transference is an instance)
- Regression – to earlier states of development
- Reaction-formation – unacceptable impulse masked by exaggeration of its opposite
- Identification – e.g. with aggressor as symbolic fulfilment of wishes
- Undoing – adoption of a pattern of behaviour which involves guilty symbolic reparation for earlier activity counter to superego

But defences are not one-sidedly pathological; social activity depends on the appropriate direction of libido, and psychoanalysis values the mature defences such as sublimation, the substitution of a socially valuable activity for a direct expression of desire, and humour, the veiled discharge of energy through a particular 'angled' perception of reality,

Psychological development is a process of redirection and transformation of libido. The history of development of the sexual drive is, according to Freud, focused in the conflict between desire and parental reality. Libido finds its focus in one bodily erotogenic zone after another. At each stage, that zone is the focus of tension and relief, and parental influence is centred on the control and socialisation of associated stages. Initially, the infant seeks gratification orally through sucking at the breast, an object for which later analogies can substitute. After the oral phase, during the second year, the struggle over toilet training shifts the child's focus to the anus. The pleasure of defecation in the **anal** stage is in conflict with parental demands for control. Fixation at or regression to one or other of these stages is supposed to be the cause of certain characteristics of personality. Third is the phallic stage, which is perhaps socially pre-eminent in importance. Because Freud took questions of male sexuality as governing his analysis of development, his account of the third phase has caused considerable disquiet – especially because of the part played by castration anxiety in the theory.

In the **phallic** stage, the relation to reality is such that family dynamics are especially important. Competition between the father and son (the son's libidinal attachment being to the mother) means that the desire has to be renounced in the light of reality because of anxiety about the father's ill-will. Freud, therefore, has the image of the person as a very radically fearful being. The situation is the *Oedipus complex*, and entails an anxiety of castration which is not supposed by Freud to be other than actual fear of actual castration, though recent analysts often take the concept to be metaphorical. The resolution of the Oedipus complex involves repression of hatred and identification with the father. Thus love arises initially as a form of obedience. The third aspect of mental functioning, superego, is developed. Notice that both ego and superego arise from the id in the sense that they involve transformations of libido.

Freud's account of child development has been criticised for being patriarchal, culture-bound, and lacking evidence. See Box 2.2 for some aspects of the psychoanalytical approach to homosexuality. The account of female development is also speculative. The female superego is supposed to be weaker, since anxiety cannot be aroused by a castration complex, and a passive personality is supposed to be developed: penis envy leads to reliance on the male. This account of female development was rejected by psychoanalysts early on as 'phallocentric'. Modern psychoanalysis has modified Freud's developmental theory considerably in the light of such findings as the importance of the mutual gaze of parent and child.

> Freud understood 'castration anxiety' in terms of the oedipal fear of the little boy that his punishment for loving his mother and so challenging his father, would be castration, and consequent relegation to what he presumes to be the position of women. While 'oedipus' is no longer thought of so literally in bodily terms, castration anxiety as a sense of powerlessness within a phallocentric society is an important theme in feminist-influenced neo-Freudian thought.
>
> (Bateman and Holmes, 1995: 236)

After a '**latency** stage', a final adaptation to society takes place in adolescence: the **genital** stage. Here, the mature adult should ideally emerge, able 'to love and to work' (i.e. enter into balanced relationships and act appropriately in social contexts)

Box 2.2 **Freud on homosexuality**

Freud took it that the infant was bisexual. The basis of an eventual homosexual orientation was to be found in the way in which the Oedipus complex was resolved so that the object of desire would be a member of one's own sex. He does *not* seem to have been particularly concerned with the widespread worry concerning the morality of male homosexuality. In a very compassionate letter to a mother, written very near the end of his life, he writes:

> I gather from your letter that your son is a homosexual. . . . Homosexuality is assuredly no advantage, but it is nothing to be ashamed of, no vice, no degradation, it cannot be classified as an illness; we consider it to be a variation of the sexual function produced by a certain arrest of sexual development.
>
> (Jones, 1964: 624)

There is no single, clear account of homosexual development, male or female, in Freud. We gather that there are several paths which might lead to this orientation. One example is given without undue neurotic strain. Sexual relationships should be possible, and a lot of libido-energy should have undergone transformation ('sublimation') into socially useful individual motives.

Criticisms

The *separability of theoretical formulations from analytical therapy* is sometimes thought possible. Certainly there is now a plethora of theoretical orientations, some of which would claim to be grounded in an account of the unconscious, but which deviate profoundly from Freud. Maybe a theory of some kind is needed to assist the therapist, but there is no fixity about what the nature of an ideal interpretative theory should be.

a paper 'On the sexual theories of children' (Freud, 1977). Here a boy, during the stage of the Oedipus complex, might be particularly affected by discovering the absence of a penis in women, the experience evoking castration anxiety particularly strongly.

> When a small boy sees his little sister's genitals . . . he does not comment on the absence of a penis but *invariably* says, as though by way of consolation and to put things right: Her —'s still quite small. But when she gets bigger it'll grow all right.' The idea of a woman with a penis returns in later life in the dreams of adults . . . If this idea of a woman with a penis becomes 'fixated' in an individual when he is a child, resisting all the influences of later life and making him as a man unable to do without a penis in his sexual object, then . . . he is bound to become a homosexual.
>
> (Freud, 1977: 193–194; emphasis and coy ellipsis in original)

In general, then, psychological causes are more important than biological ones in the Freudian account of homosexuality.

There is ***diversity and fluidity*** in psychoanalytical theory. New ideas relating to an original concept tend to be tagged on, leading to a kind of cluster of meanings. Each of these clusters is doubtless suggestive, and provides insights of a poetic kind. But there is lack of hard clarity. Maybe the use of a theory in therapeutic practice demands such fluidity and poetic resonance.

The question is often raised concerning the empirical justification of Freudian theory. ***What is its scientific status?*** Some epistemologists (i.e. philosophers interested in the question of how claims to *know* can be justified) have argued that the key feature of science was that its claims were *testable*. Popper (1959) refined this by demarcating science from non-science by arguing that scientific statements were 'tenable and refutable'. It should be clear what kind of evidence would show them to be false.

Now, there may be an *in principle* problem with the falsifiability of at least some propositions of psychoanalysis (focusing now on the causal claims of the 'energetics' aspect of the theory). For instance, it might be said that the anal character is obstinate, punctual, somewhat mean (parsimonious), orderly/tidy, and irritable. But what if the mode of toilet training held to develop this character structure did not in fact do so in an individual case? Would this disconfirm the hypothesis? No, it is possible, instead, to argue that we have here an example of a *reaction-formation*. This defence mechanism has led to the person expressing the reverse traits – in effect, anal eroticism is being expressed by the traits of mildness, happy-go-luckiness, generosity and good-humour. If so, we have no way of testing the basic model – whatever the outcome in terms of personality, the model can account for it.

Freudian ***hermeneutics of suspicion*** may be overdone. The hermeneutics of meaning-recollection is carried out on the basis of a faith in the person's view of their world. Not that it is true in the sense of being objective – all experience is from a particular viewpoint. But true in the sense that *this is actually what the world is like for them*. Here we have the phenomenological approach in psychology (Giorgi, 1970; van den Berg, 1972). Unlike the hermeneutics of suspicion, the standpoint of the interpretation is *within* the world-view of the person. Freudian analysis challenges the viewpoint of the individual and provides a critique – but on what basis? Freudian theory is intended primarily to assist interpretation, bringing together a very wide range of problematical aspects of a person's thought, attitudes, phantasies, dreams and behaviour under some umbrella of understanding. But wouldn't other 'story lines' be as helpful? Certain modern analysts (e.g. Schafer, 1983) do suggest just that.

The Freudian ***critique of consciousness*** – the denial, in the hermeneutics of suspicion, that the individual's account of their experience is true – requires that the alternative account provided by the psychoanalyst be very fully supported by evidence. The coherence of the psychoanalyst's alternative account in contrast to the puzzling nature of the analysand's own account may be good evidence, but in the end it is the persuasiveness of the interpretation that counts. Does the analysand accept the new view of their experience and revise their understanding accordingly? But if they do, is this acceptance 'real', or is it a sign that they have been socialised into the way of thinking of psychoanalysis?

Summary

What is Freud's understanding of human nature? We will address the question by means of the set of categories outlined in the Introduction:

- *Consciousness.* A secondary mental phenomenon which has the function of providing the individual with an awareness of 'reality' to the extent that desires can be expressed and satisfied within the world.
- *The self.* The ego is not entirely conscious because its scope extends into the unconscious realm of the defence mechanisms. We are essentially deeply fearful (especially of the outer world of other people), but also deeply moved by desires (which arise from within but need other people for their satisfaction). The self is partly the site and partly the

consequence of these conflicts. Selfhood is severely limited in Freud: for the most part we do not ourselves know why we act in the way we do.

- *The body.* This is primary for Freud. We start our mental life as undifferentiated id. The unconscious is irrational and not directly accessible largely because it is not structured in the categories of consciousness or reality, but is bodily – and a matter of feeling. However, insight into aspects of the unconscious can give us increasing personal control over our behaviour.
- *Other people.* Others constitute both the source of threat and the locus of desire. It is important to note that all relationships can be taken as repetitions of the original system of relationships within the socialising unit – normally the family. Thus others take on irrational meanings such as the father figure, the rival sibling, the all-consuming mother, etc.
- *The physical world.* In so far as this has relevance for Freud, it again reflects the family nexus (because this is where a person's perceptual categories developed). So psychoanalysts might take the 'mother earth' metaphor seriously.

Further Reading

Freud's writing is clear and elegant, and the innumerable secondary sources are needed for commentary rather than clarification. *The Standard Edition of the Complete Psychological Works of Sigmund Freud* (Hogarth Press and the Institute of Psycho-Analysis, from 1953) is the authoritative English translation. The *Pelican Freud Library* may be more accessible, and is based on the *Standard Edition*. It is to that edition that citations in the chapter refer. One might start with the following:

Lectures 21 and 22 from *Introductory Lectures on Psychoanalysis* (Volume 1, 1974), about psychological development.

The Interpretation of Dreams (Volume 4, 1976), which has, as its final chapter, 'The psychology of the dream-processes'. This is Freud's extremely interesting attempt to combine the two approaches of his theory.

On Metapsychology: The Theory of Psychoanalysis (Volume 11, 1984).

'An outline of psychoanalysis', from *Historical and Expository Works on Psychoanalysis* (Volume 15, 1986), which gives overviews of the theory as Freud formulated it at various times in its development.

Chapter 3

An inner world: cognitive psychology

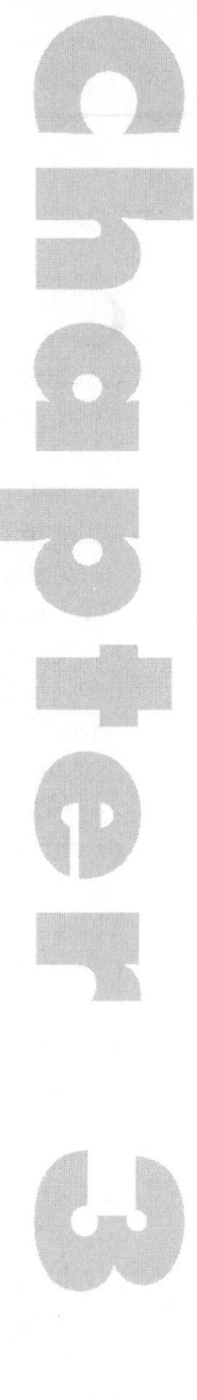

COGNITION INCLUDES PERCEPTION, remembering, thinking, reasoning, imagining and learning. Psychology is, for cognitive psychologists, a biological science, but uncovering biological bases of cognition in brain mechanisms is not the only way in which outside support is marshalled in order to give weight to psychological models of mental functioning. Of equal significance is the interplay between psychology and computer science. Views concerning mental functioning are sometimes elaborated as computer programs – the idea being that such demonstrations show the feasibility of the claim that *this* is how the mind works. The link between cognitive psychology, neuroscience, and computer science – together with aspects of philosophy and linguistics – is so close that the term 'cognitive science' is often given to the whole group.

Unlike the topics of other chapters, the view of cognitive psychology concerning human nature cannot be tackled through the analysis of the work of one person or even a few people. There are historically key authors, certainly, but – and this is typical of developed sciences in general – cognitive psychology is characterised by a very large and diverse body of research studies. If anywhere in psychology and related disciplines, it is in cognitive psychology that we find a *paradigm* (Kuhn, 1970). By 'paradigm' is meant a strong and accepted perspective on the nature of a discipline and its subject matter, together with a widely agreed approach to investigation, so that there are well-understood criteria of acceptable research. In analysing cognitive psychology, then, I will be drawing attention to basic assumptions which have the status, amongst cognitive psychologists themselves, of 'common sense'. In particular, cognitive psychologists take for granted that the processes that interest them are definite, actual factual events in the real world. Regarding these things, there is an underlying non-negotiable, solid truth or reality about which it is possible to attain ever more accurate approximate knowledge.

Scientific progress takes place as the community of cognitive psychologists develop models of this reality which are more and more adequate in picturing these facts.

In accordance with this assumption, cognitive psychology adopts a *positivist* approach to its research. The purpose of science is to model the mental realm in its theories. The theories will show how certain 'variables' (that is, distinct measurable entities) interrelate, especially how they relate to each other in a cause-and-effect fashion. Mathematical formulations of the relationships between variables are to be sought if at all possible. Research activity involves testing hypotheses regarding relationships between variables, and gradually developing scientific laws of mental processes.

Now, though this set of assumptions certainly appears to be commonsensical (humans do perceive and think, don't they?), it will nevertheless be seen in Chapters 6 and 7 that the assumptions are in fact controversial. It could be, for instance, that, while 'perceiving' and 'thinking' relate strongly to the place human beings have in our contemporary culture, quite different notions of mental life may be possible – and in fact in the next chapter we see that Skinner has indeed developed a significantly divergent understanding of human nature, and one which is even critical of the use of 'mental' terms at all.

What cognitive psychology is trying to do

Cognitive psychology aims to ***model the mental processes of 'cognition'***; that is, of perceiving, remembering, thinking, reasoning and language use. Human cognition is viewed in terms of ***information processing***, whereby there is a sequential flow starting with the sensing of an object or event and ending up with the use, storage in memory, or loss of the information.

A ***constructivist*** view is taken of human mental activity; that is, the process of cognition leads to the building of mental conceptualisations in terms of which a person thinks and acts. Therefore a distinction can be made, within cognitive psychological work, between the modelling of *cognitive processes* and the uncovering of *personal cognitions*. Cognitive psychologists' own ***models of cognition are constructions***. But there is a limit to this relativism. It is assumed that the mental processes under investigation do have a solid reality to which scientific models gradually begin to conform. So, although the distinction between the 'inner world' of cognition and an 'outer reality' does seem to run the risk of ***dualism***, cognitive psychologists regard their subject matter as a unity. It is supposed that there are laws governing the construction of the inner world, so the inner world is fully dependent on the physical world and not of a different order of reality.

This chapter is structured in terms of the distinction between the modelling of cognitive processes and the uncovering of personal cognitions.

The cognitive processes

An early cognitivist, Kenneth Craik (1943) made very explicit the idea that cognitive activity is to be regarded as a process of forming an internal model of external reality. On the basis of such 'symbolisation', reasoning can take place:

> the function of such symbolisation is plain. If the organism carries a 'small scale model' of external reality and of its own possible actions within its head, it is able to try out various alternatives, conclude which is the best of them, react to future situations before they arise, utilise the knowledge of past events in dealing with the present and future, and in every way to react in a much fuller, safer, and more competent manner to the emergencies which face it.
>
> (Craik, 1943: 61)

There was significant work using what we now recognise as the cognitive approach well before the Second World War (an outstanding example is Bartlett [1932], whose work also shows the intimate connection between cognitivism and constructionism).

But the dominance of behaviourism, especially in the United States, from, say, 1930 to 1960, inhibited research involving the 'symbolisation' of mental processes.

Behaviourism had eschewed any reference to mental events because they were seen as being unobservable and not open to definitive test. (The methodological behaviourism I am referring to here must be distinguished from Skinner's viewpoint, which does *not* reject the study of mental processes on methodological grounds but for conceptual reasons detailed in the next chapter.) However, the modelling of mental processes by cognitivists avoided the methodological criticism. For example, subtle differences in human performance when a person is presented with particular differences in the stimulus situation enable the researcher to make inferences about the working of the mental apparatus. It was the advent of control engineering and information sciences that led to behaviourism's loss of dominance, for these sciences provided a range of vocabularies with which to represent higher mental processes in a precise manner amenable to mathematisation.

The leading figures in the early computer simulation of thinking were Newell *et al.* (e.g. 1961), who studied the strategies used by people in their thinking, and then translated these into programs. The programs represented the researchers' understanding of the human processes, and the actual preformance of computer and human could be compared in order to test the adequacy of the theoretical model. Thus the modelling of mental processes can still be regarded as *methodologically behaviourist*.

The sequence of cognitive processes

Cognition as information processing. Mental activity is seen as a flow of information, maybe originating with sensory input and ending up as an internal representation of the world (perhaps committed to memory).

Within behaviourism, developments in a cognitive direction were made from time to time. Perhaps Miller *et al.*'s (1960) *Plans and the Structure of Behaviour* is the most obvious, in that the authors termed themselves 'cognitive behaviourists'. One tendency was for writers to attempt to preserve the behaviourist enterprise of describing human activity as the lawful response to environmental conditions while introducing some 'inner' processes which would intervene in the path between stimulus and response.

For instance, in an attempt to defend a behaviourist account of the acquisition of language in infants (which had come under devastating criticism, notably by Chomsky in 1959), Mowrer (1960) argued that 'meaning' could be understood to be a 'mediating response' (r_m). This would allow for a person to learn a word (which, for behaviourists, meant that they had been conditioned to respond in a particular way to it) and also, at the same time, to have learned an inner response which would have a more general effect, enabling the person to associate the word with other things to which the meaning applied. Here we do seem to have the beginnings of a cognitive behaviourism, since the meaning is somehow detached from the strict determinism of a specifiable stimulus–response learning situation (how is unclear), and a mental process intervenes.

However, Fodor (1965) showed that, if behavioural psychology required that human behaviour be predictable from a knowledge of the history of reinforcement, then a mediating response would have itself to be specifically conditioned in some way – its 'detachment' from the main process of conditioning is not explicable otherwise. Meaning cannot be an r_m if the behaviourist model is to be maintained.

It seems from this history that behaviourism cannot become cognitive – allowing relatively autonomous mental processes to exist which disturb the determinative effect of conditioning – and retain its nature. And we shall see in Chapter 4 that Skinner would agree with this conclusion.

In the UK, the dominance of behaviourism was felt, but it was not uncontested. A strong proto-cognitivist development was the 'skills' approach. Here the idea of mediation ('organisation of behaviour') between stimulus and response is necessary. Figure 3.1 is based on Welford's (1968) diagram of the major cognitive processes in the chain from stimulus to response.

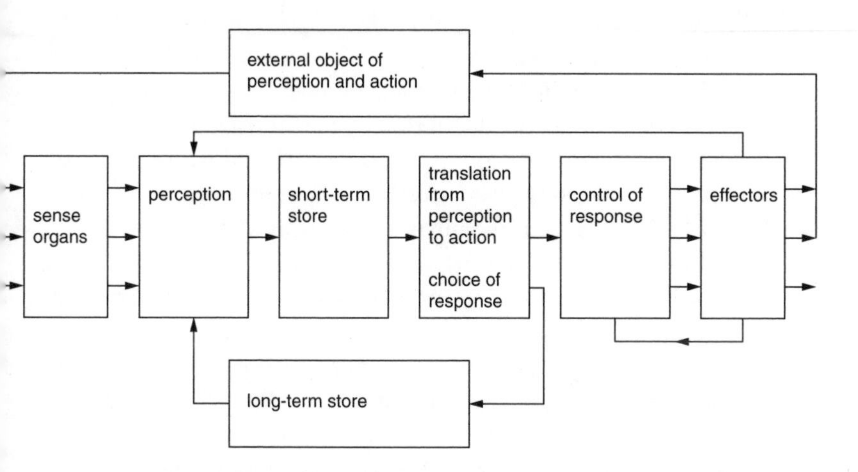

Figure 3.1 **Block diagram of human sensory-motor system (after Welford, 1968)**

Welford emphasised that the diagram only showed a few of the many feedback loops which exist (p. 19). The fact that, nevertheless, he did choose to show the effect of the 'long-term store' (i.e. memory based on past experience) on perception is significant.

In Figure 3.1, physical stimulation at the senses is taken to be 'meaningless', for meaning is something which is added to the stimulus when it is interpreted. To interpret stimulation, past experience which is accumulated in the 'long-term store' is brought to bear on it. So perception is understood by Welford (and he is representative of cognitive psychologists in this) as a process by which the person interprets incoming sensory information by the use of accumulated experience and renders it meaningful.

Having been perceived – that is, rendered significant (and this is not necessarily a conscious process) – the information enters a short-term store. This 'consists of some kind of brain *activity*' (Welford, 1968: 197). Although cognitivists might regard it as begging too many questions, 'focal consciousness' would not be too wild a term for this stage in the processing of information.

Besides involving active, conscious attention, short-term memory has the characteristics of restricted capacity and susceptibility to interference – especially when similar sounds to those of verbal information being retained are introduced. The short-term retention of an unfamiliar telephone number, for instance, is notoriously open to annoying disruption by one hearing other numbers. And it does seem that 'coding' in the short-term store is verbal-acoustic, even when the 'raw stuff' being stored is originally visual. Retention is enhanced by subvocal rehearsal of the material.

Short-term retention is linked by Welford to problem-solving and thinking, and these associated stages – together with the 'programming of action' (1968: 238) when this is not a matter of automatic processes – have in common what a non-cognitivist would unblushingly refer to as awareness. We will consider the coyness of cognitivists over the issue of consciousness in the next section, but it is worth noting Welford's attempt to treat complex mental processes in terms of machine analogies:

> it is attractive and provocative to conceive of thinking as akin to the operation of a computer going through a series of stages in each of which data are taken either from the sense organs or from a memory store to be combined with other data in some sort of computation, and the result is stored temporarily to be used later with other data in a further computation, and so on.
>
> (Welford, 1968: 237)

I have introduced the stages of cognitive processing through Welford's diagram, though this may be seen as dated. The reason is that later authors, in attempting to give the kind of broad picture of cognition necessary for a book like the current one, have not been so explicit concerning the 'stages'. Partly, the complexity of the system that emerges as a result of the vast number of significant papers which have been published in the third of a century since Welford, makes such a summary diagram well-nigh impossible.

In Figure 3.2 I have nevertheless attempted a synthesis of *some* of the modelling which has taken place regarding the initial stages of cognition. First of all, it is worth pointing out the way

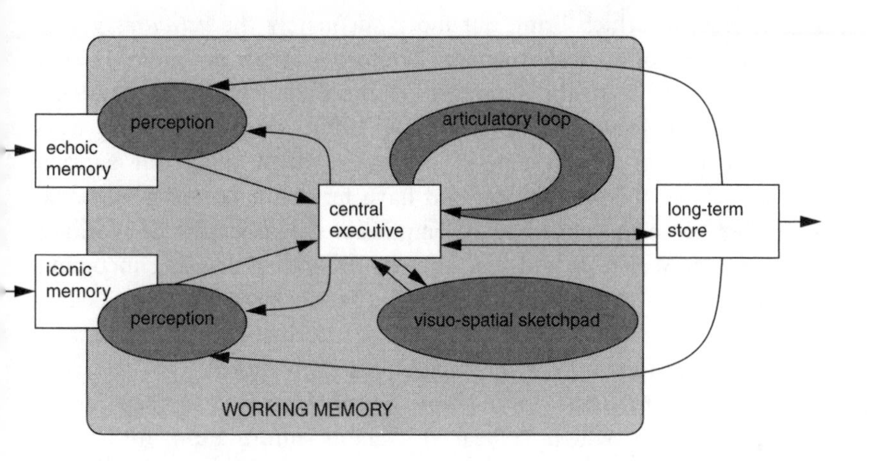

Figure 3.2 **Some cognitive processes associated with 'working memory'**

This diagram includes processes discussed by Neisser (1967), Baddeley (1986) and Logie (1995).

in which the entry of information has been elaborated. Neisser's (1967) very influential account, *Cognitive Psychology*, devoted a great deal of space to the way in which, quite prior to conscious intervention, sensory information was held in very short-term storage, separately, it seems, for each modality. After the cessation of a sound or sight, information about it is briefly available for retrieval from so-called 'echoic' and 'iconic' memory (whether there are equivalent 'buffer' stores for other sense modalities is less clear). Yet these stores have particular characteristics above and beyond simply comprising lingering after-sensations. The retrievability of the information can be lost due to the effects on the store of later sensation. And the sensation is not retrieved 'raw': it is already processed in the sense of having been rendered meaningful through, it seems, the activity of long-term memory on the information. Perception, at a simple level, has already begun. We are never aware of the raw sensation.

Recent writers have found it necessary, in the light of accumulated findings, to replace Welford's short-term store with a set of notions which bring out more adequately the *activities* which this stage of cognition entails. Welford's earlier account stressed, as we have seen, the dynamism of the short-term store. Baddeley and his colleagues (e.g. Baddeley, 1990) are among those who have proposed a system of processes which bring out various aspects of this dynamism, and have termed it *working memory*. They are also concerned to emphasise the functions of working memory which do not just have to do with processing incoming perceptions and passing them on to be dealt with in later cognitive stages but also with active use of information in thinking and reasoning (developing the suggestions of Welford).

The *articulatory (or phonological) loop* is an explication of the way in which 'rehearsal' retains information for active processing. The *visuo-spatial sketch pad* provides something of an analogy of the articulatory loop for non-verbal material, reflecting the finding that individuals can work with imagery. In effect, recent modelling reflects the fact that the 'active present' comprises information which is represented cognitively in at least the two modalities of verbal/acoustic and imaged/spatial awareness.

The core of working memory, according to Baddeley, is a *central executive*. Welford's speculative machine analogy for thinking is embodied in this component, for it would be the central executive which would actually perform such tasks as bringing up information 'to be combined with other data in some sort of computation, and the result is stored temporarily to be used later'.

The models discussed so far merely mention long-term memory. Yet important early work was done on long-term memory. Bartlett's *Remembering* (1932) showed general principles at work in the recall of stories and pictures. The overriding factor was the effect of 'effort after meaning' whereby parts of stories which stretched the understanding of his research participants were not recalled, or were recalled in a conventionalised form. A related observation in the recall of simple drawings was that the reproduction would be affected by the way the picture had been verbally tagged. Effort after meaning is a pervasive principle of 'every cognitive reaction – perceiving, imaging, remembering, thinking and reasoning' (ibid.: 44). It is not necessarily conscious; it entails the assimilation of an element of cognition to some pattern: The 'pre-formed setting, scheme, or pattern is utilised in a completely unanalytical and unwitting manner' (ibid.: 45). But what is meant by setting, scheme, or situation?

> Psychologically, a situation always involves the arrangement of cognitive material by some more or less specific action tendency, or group of tendencies, and to define a situation in any given case we have to refer, not only to the arrangement of material, but also to the particular activity or activities in operation.
>
> (Bartlett, 1932: 231)

So the organisation of memory (and other cognitive processes) is in terms of the meaningful interrelationship of memorial 'elements', constellated around situations, settings or schemata which are activities or tendencies of the individual.

The processes of memory are describable in terms of laws that lead to a picture of memorial processes as *constructive*. Bartlett firmly rejected the idea that memory is a storehouse of the traces of past events, experiences, or reactions, laid down at the time and preserved until recalled. One difficulty with the idea of memory as consisting of traces of specific events is that 'every normal individual must carry about with him an incalculable number of individual traces' (1932: 197). In contrast to this, his own findings indicated that 'the past operates as an organised mass rather than as a group of elements each of which retains its special character' (ibid.: 197). Just as recent research has re-emphasised the active nature of the short-term store, or working memory, so Bartlett leads us to see long-term memory as dynamic – organised by meaning.

Recent experimental work on long-term memory has noted different forms of memory. It is not necessarily the case that remembering story-like material or pictorial images is the same as remembering 'facts', events or such things as how to drive a car. The major distinction that has been drawn is between *propositional* knowledge and *procedural* knowledge (being able to state something and being able to perform some physical action). It was Tulving (1983) who made this distinction as regards memory. He further distinguished between two forms of propositional knowledge: episodic and semantic. The former is to do with personal biographical events; the latter with information or other material which is not dependent on the personal circumstances of its acquisition for its significance.

How these different kinds of knowledge may relate to cognitive systems is controversial. It is of interest here, however, that the study of the semantic memory takes up, in a rather abstract form, the idea of organisation through meaning. Bartlett, however, stressed the personal meaningfulness – schemata and situations – underlying recall, and did so in a way which would definitely bring episodic and semantic memory together. Current research on semantic memory (e.g. Rosch and Lloyd, 1978) attempts to describe networks of similarity and dissimilarity among sets of concepts, often arranging these in hierarchical structures. Rosch takes the view that the environment is experienced in terms of coincidences of attributes, and perception and memory follow suit. For instance, some concepts are linked together in similarity, and are all members of a particular category: wren, robin and sparrow – birds. Plainly, this is a psychological version of taxonomy, and the claim is that the mental furniture of individuals is a personal taxonomy, at least as far as semantic memory is concerned. We will see this view carried through in a somewhat different context in Kelly's theory of personal constructs.

This outline of the sequence of cognitive processes, and the sketch of the way in which psychologists have elaborated the description of short-term and long-term storage, will have to suffice. I believe it accurately represents the way in which cognitive psychology develops its portrayal of human nature. Studies of thinking, reasoning, etc., pursue the same tendencies of research: the outcomes of experimental studies are interpreted in terms of algorithms which lay out, in the clearest achievable way, the procedures a machine would have to follow were it to reproduce the human behaviour.

Agency and consciousness

In reiterating, towards the end of the book, his rejection of the idea of remembering as involving the re-excitation of traces, and insisting on the activity of the individual in *constructing* the memory, Bartlett wrote that such construction is guided by a personal orientation to the material to be recalled, which is 'an effect of the organism's capacity to turn round upon its own "schemata", and is directly a function of consciousness' (1932: 213). In other words, the individual makes a decision in constructing the memory, a decision motivated by the meanings of the material to be remembered in relation to their current attitude. Bartlett credits this theory with the virtue of giving 'to consciousness a definite function other than the mere fact of being aware' (ibid.: 214).

Bartlett's stance here is of great interest because it indicates that individuals are active in remembering (they are *agents*), and that there is a choice in the material and manner of recall. Consciousness provides the individual with the capacity to 'turn round on their own schemata' – i.e. to consider the less-than-perfectly structured material – and organise it into a 'memory'.

In noting Welford's attempt to treat complex mental processes in terms of machine analogies rather than by the use of the everyday terminology of thinking, I referred to the general coyness of cognitivists concerning consciousness. Hesitations in the literature over Baddeley's 'central executive' seem to stem from the concern that this function may not be open to modelling, for it suggests conscious activity. The problem with consciousness as an element in a cognitive model is that it appears to demand a loosening of the determinism which modelling requires.

Individual cognitions: Kelly's Personal Construct Theory

So far, I have concentrated on the cognitivist account of the way in which information is processed mentally. The other mode of cognitivist thinking – while not entirely ignoring such information-processing – nevertheless focuses on the product of such processing: personal cognitions.

George A. Kelly is usually viewed as a clear example of the cognitive approach in psychology. It needs to be pointed out that this is not the only reading of Kelly. Maher's edited collection of Kelly's papers (1969) shows an emphasis on behaviour rather than the mental aspects of construing (see also Burr and Butt, 1992). However, it does seem that, for Kelly, the person acts not in accordance with the way the world actually is but according to his or her 'construction' of it. To this extent his work is cognitivist. For Kelly, the 'Fundamental Postulate' expresses this: '*A person's processes are psychologically channellised by the way in which he* [sic] *anticipates events.*'

What, specifically, Kelly was trying to do

Kelly put forward a specific version of the objectives of cognitive psychologists. An initial orientation was to view the person as acting as an ***informal scientist*** who views the world ('events') by way of categories of interpretation ('constructs') which are open to modification in the light of experience. In adopting this model, he treated the individual as 'naturally active' (so a theory of motivation of the usual kind is not useful); the ***direction*** in which they chose to develop their activity is the matter of interest. Since reappraisal of this direction is thought possible, by conscious reflection on their construction of the world, this part of the theory is labelled '***constructive alternativism***'.

Kelly intended to model some aspects of ***social activity***, believing that an approach to understanding can be made by comparing the actors' construct systems. As an aid to this and other investigations – for therapy or research – a ***logical scheme*** by which the researcher might specify in an organised way individuals' construct systems was sought; one which would facilitate assessment without sacrificing either individuality or changeability.

The formal theory

The theory which embodies Kelly's aims is laid out, roughly in keeping with the original (gender insensitive) language of *A Theory of Personal Constructs* (1955), in Box 3.1.

The fundamental postulate is the core assumption of cognitive theory generally: the activity of a person is not a direct response to the 'objective' situation, but arises rather from the person's construction of the current events. Such a construction is based on the representations of this category of event which have been built up from past experience (Corollary 7).

The structure of construct systems. Some corollaries deal with the common structure which it is supposed all 'construct systems' have, for, although Corollary 2 tells us that individuals differ in their construction of events, the actual structure of construct systems is supposed, at the most abstract level, to be universal. Construct systems are ordered hierarchically (Corollary 3) – there being more general constructs which can be broken down into more specific ones. And each construct is treated as bipolar; since good carries with it as part of its meaning not bad; 'good–bad' is a bipolar construct (Corollary 4). Corollary 8 tells us that constructs, and therefore the systems of which they are a part, differ in their flexibility. Some apply to a very wide range of events, others are very specific.

The construing of events. Kelly is explicit that the individual may be faced with a situation which is outside the scope of their understanding (it seems that an event can be perceived in some way, but the person realises that they cannot adequately construe it); moreover, a given construct is only relevant for certain events (Corollary 6). The theory allows for the lack of pure logic in human cognition, since Corollary 9 makes it explicit that a person can be found to view one event in a way that seems to contradict their construction of another event which, to the outsider, seems equivalent. How the person actually uses the construct system is indicated in Corollary 5. It is put rather oddly. In perceiving an event, the person chooses to construe it in a way that makes for 'the greater possibility for extension and definition of his system'.

Box 3.1 **Kelly's formal theory**

	Postulate and corollaries	*Definitions*
	Fundamental postulate	A person's processes are psychologically channellised by the ways in which he anticipates events
1	Construction corollary	A person anticipates events by construing their replications
2	Individuality corollary	Persons differ from each other in their construction of events
3	Organisation corollary	Each person characteristically evolves, for his convenience in anticipating events, a construction system embracing ordinal relationships between constructs
4	Dichotomy corollary	A person's construct system is composed of a finite number of dichotomous constructs
5	Choice corollary	A person chooses for himself that alternative in a dichotomised construct through which he anticipates the greater possibility for extension and definition of his system

So the occurrence of an event is not just categorised using the construct which is most ready-to-hand, even if the fit is rough and ready. Rather, the event is used to develop distinctions and elaborations in the system of cognition itself. In this way, Kelly allows for both forms of cognitive development which Piaget (1977) described: *assimilation*, in which the new experience is dealt with in terms of a way of thinking or acting already in existence, and

Postulate and corollaries		*Definitions*
6	Range corollary	A construct is convenient for the anticipation of a finite range of events only
7	Experience corollary	A person's construction system varies as he successively construes the replications of events
8	Modulation corollary	The variation in a person's construction system is limited by the permeability of the constructs within whose range of convenience the variants lie
9	Fragmentation corollary	A person may successively employ a variety of construction subsystems which are inferentially incompatible with each other
10	Commonality corollary	To the extent that one person employs a construction of experience which is similar to that employed by another, his psychological processes are similar to that of the other person
11	Sociality corollary	To the extent that one person construes the construction processes of another, he may play a part in a social process involving the other person

accommodation, in which thought or action is altered in a manner appropriate to the novel experience.

The individual and others. The Individuality Corollary, which has already been mentioned, might make it seem that each construct system had unique contents, and that therefore an individual's construction of an event would be quite idiosyncratic and unpredictable. In fact, Corollaries 10 and 11 provide constraints

***Box 3.2* Cognitive theory and homosexuality**

If we look to research on *cognitive mental processes* for findings concerning homosexuality, we will find ourselves disappointed. Even subtle aspects of the processing of information are unlikely to vary with sexual orientation – and if such a discovery were made, it is unclear what its meaning would be. But the other aspect of cognitive research, that which looks at *actual cognitions*, does provide the beginnings of an approach to sexual orientation.

Kelly would expect, in the welter of constructs and elements of a person's construct system, a mapping of the interpersonal attitudes and preferences – some sexual – which would at least describe the 'mental world' of an individual homosexual. By definition, sexual orientation is likely to be seen in the way a person construes individuals on the construct 'attractive to me'.

There is no theory of the *development* of sexual orientation (gay or straight), but at least Construct Theory can provide us with links, in an individual case, between the sexual realm and the other dimensions of the construed environment. Given that homosexuality – particularly male homosexuality – remains only patchily accepted in our society currently, signs of denial and signs that the person disavows the self-concept 'homosexual' may also be found – the cognitive consequences of social stigma. A disrupted system of personal constructs may therefore occur, with accompanying emotional distress. At the psychological level, the question is one of self-acceptance.

on individuality. It would be a matter of empirical research to find out the extent to which a particular group of people shared constructs in common, but a shared language is at least one major reason to suppose a great deal of commonality – and commonality means shared mental processes according to Kelly. The Sociality Corollary allows for the individual to include within their system of cognition, knowledge of the perspectives of other people though these may not be shared by the individual themselves. To interact with another person, of course, requires knowledge of this sort.

It is important to mention that *self* is, for Kelly, a construct like any other. And the individual's construction of their own personal attributes will be included within the construct system along with their constructions of the attributes of others. In this sense, I am an object of my own cognition – a matter that is developed in great detail by Sartre, as we shall see in Chapter 5.

In Box 3.2 I indicate the way in which Kelly's approach would deal with our thematic example of homosexuality.

Change in construing and the emotions

Kelly dealt with the emotions of anxiety, hostility, guilt, threat, fear and aggression. They were taken to be *constructs about the state of the construct system*. Emotions relate to the awareness that the system is in some transitional state or other. So in anxiety, events which confront the person are 'mostly outside the range of convenience' of his or her construct system:

> We become anxious when we can only partially construe the events which we encounter and too many of their implications are obscure. Sex for the chaste, adulthood for the adolescent, power for the humble and death for nearly all of us tend to provoke anxiety. It is the *unknown* aspects of things that go bump in the night that give them their potency.
>
> (Bannister and Fransella, 1971: 35)

The thing to notice is that the emotions seem to require two levels of cognition, construing in the direct sense but also awareness of the state of the construct system and its relationship to the 'outside world'. In some ways this account of the emotions constitutes a difficulty with the theory, for knowledge of the 'outer world', which seems necessary to evaluate the state of the construct system, seems only to be obtainable through the construct system itself.

Related to this is the problem that, if all our awareness is in terms of the system of constructs, how is information that challenges the current constructs registered? How, therefore, can change occur? And how is 'constructive alternativism' made possible? An explicit theory of consciousness seems to be necessary.

Criticisms

Objection may be raised concerning the ***artificiality of models*** of cognitive processes and of cognitions. In this vein, the modelling of cognitive processes is regarded as unsatisfactory by humanistic psychologists. It can be seen to presuppose a mechanistic view of human nature. Similarly, in theories of the Kellian kind, the representation of the furniture of the mind is by way of a model of semantic knowledge which provides an over-organised, over-articulate and unduly verbal account of the psychological realm.

The role of consciousness in the cognitive approach is ambiguous. Bartlett and Kelly both see consciousness in terms of reflection and choice. In Baddeley's account of working memory, the central executive is plainly synonymous with consciousness. Yet there is no explicit account of consciousness (if it is acknowledged). It is odd for such a major phenomenon to be taken for granted when such minutiae as the kind of coding in long-term memory is treated with enormous care.

There is a certain ***dualism*** in cognitivist theory. Dualism in this context refers to the radical separation between a mental, subjective, private world and an outer, material, public world. Neisser (1967) specifically asserts a dualistic cognitive view:

> There certainly is a real world . . . However, we have no direct *im*mediate access to the world, nor to any of its properties. . . . Whatever we know about reality has been *mediated*, not only by the organs of sense but by complex systems which interpret and reinterpret sensory information.
>
> (Neisser, 1967: 3)

The behaviourist B.F. Skinner, whose extreme anti-dualism I describe in the next chapter, responds directly to this 'illusion of a double world':

> Suppose someone were to coat the occipital lobes of the brain with a special photographic emulsion which, when developed, yielded a reasonable copy of a current visual stimulus. In many quarters this would be regarded as a triumph in the physiology of vision. Yet nothing could be more disastrous, for we should have to start all over again and ask how the organism sees a picture in its occipital cortex. . . . It is most convenient, for both organism and psychophysiologist if the external world is never copied – if the world we know is simply the world around us. The same may be said of theories according to which the brain interprets signals sent to it and in some sense reconstructs external stimuli. If the real world is, indeed, scrambled in transmission but later reconstructed in the brain, we must then start all over again and explain how the organism sees the reconstruction.
>
> (Skinner, 1964: 87)

Cognitive psychology generally suffers from the fact that, when the attempt is made to model the 'inner' *subjective representation* of an aspect of the 'outer' world adequately, we find that all the complexity of the outer world has to be imported to the mind.

Summary

What is cognitive psychology's understanding of human nature? I address the question by means of the usual set of categories.

- *Consciousness*. As a process, being conscious is having the capacity to construe the world. Consciousness of some event is governed by the schemata or constructs by which it is represented mentally. But 'constructive alternativism', and equivalent notions of cognitive choice, indicates that the individual can revise their construction of events – whether this is done 'at will' or not is left inexplicit.

- *The self*. There is no specific place for a 'self' in models of cognitive processes. Bartlett (1932: 309) almost triumphantly set aside the hypothesis of a 'substantial unitary Self, lurking behind all experience'. Self is a *concept*, subject to construction processes like anything else in one's world. One's self-concept is of great importance, but has no different *kind* of representation within the cognitive system.
- *The body*. The body is an element or complex set of elements within one's world. Cognitive psychology does not presuppose any special relationship one might have with one's own body.
- *Other people*. There is no particular theoretical reason within cognitive psychology for other people to be regarded as being of any different status to objects of the physical world. That there are very central and elaborate constructs or schemata regarding people may be because of their importance to the individual's welfare, and the predominance of others in the significant events of everyday experience.
- *The physical world* is responded to in a way which is determined by one's construction of it. One does not act 'directly' in response to the 'objective' features of the world, but via one's construal of the world.

Further reading

A number of eminent researchers in cognitive psychology have provided summaries of the field. The earliest is Neisser, U. (1967) *Cognitive Psychology*, New York: Appleton-Century-Crofts. More recent are:

Anderson, J.R. (1990) *Cognitive Psychology and its Implications* (3rd edn), New York: Freeman.

Lindsay, P.H. and Norman, D.A. (1972) *Human Information Processing. An Introduction to Psychology*, New York: Academic Press.
Hampson, P.J. and Morris, P.E. (1996) *Understanding Cognition*, Oxford: Blackwell.

Virtually all general texts on personality have some reference to Kelly's work (not always understood to be cognitive).

Kelly, G.A. (1955) *The Psychology of Personal Constructs* (2 vols), New York: Norton [reprinted, 1991, London: Routledge].
Bannister, D. and Fransella, F. (1986) *Inquiring Man: The Theory of Personal Constructs* (3rd edn), London: Routledge.
Burr, V. and Butt, T. (1992) *Invitation to Personal Construct Psychology*, London: Whurr.

Chapter 4

chapter 4

. . . Not separable from the world: Skinner's radical behaviourism

HISTORICALLY, COGNITIVE PSYCHOLOGY emerged as a critique of *methodological* behaviourism – the idea that mental processes could not be the object of scientific study because they were not open to observation. Cognitive psychology began to insist on the reality of inner processes, leading to studies of perception, memory, thinking and so on. But Skinner's is not a methodological behaviourism. He is quite willing to discuss thinking, perceiving and the rest. His viewpoint constitutes a critique of the cognitivist approach to these things, specifically its dualism. The best description of the 'inside of the head' is that chemical and electrical events occur there in darkness. It is certainly not the place to look for the basic features of human nature. So it is right to consider Skinner's behaviourism as a contemporary critique of cognitivism – and one which leads naturally to the later chapters.

B.F. Skinner (1904–1990) kept informal notebooks of his opinions and interpretations on a very wide range of matters. These jottings (Skinner, *Notebooks*, 1980) are of great interest from our point of view, since they show the author trying to understand daily occurrences within his own framework. An entry in that book sets the scene for our investigation of Skinner's approach to human nature. He asserts (Skinner, 1980: 333) that he did not write his book *Beyond Freedom and Dignity* (1971)! Rather, he argues that it is simply the product of his genetic endowment and personal history 'working *through*' him. What can this mean? Of course Skinner was the author of the book. His name is on the spine and there is no suggestion that it was plagiarised. But what Skinner is saying is that any person is continuous with the web of causes and effects in the world as a whole, and the attempt of psychology to separate out the 'psyche' and its activity is misplaced. Furthermore, the person is not an originator of 'their' activity, but is to be seen simply as the place where a very wide range of variables interplay. Nobody, in this sense, was the author of *Beyond Freedom and Dignity*.

What Skinner was trying to do

Skinner's is a ***materialist psychology***. Though psychology is a biological science it is beside the point to wait for results from studies of inner bodily mechanisms before setting out to investigate behaviour. The person is an intrinsic part of the flow of causes and effects in the material world as a whole, and so interest should be turned away from the 'interior' of the individual; or, rather, interior and exterior are equally parts of the world.

A jotting from the *Notebooks* puts his point of view pointedly. In commentary on a case of mass murder, Skinner notes the fact that the murderer was found to have a brain tumour. But he rejects the idea that the tumour was the cause of the criminal behaviour.

> The boy's father unwittingly got closer to the real causes. He described himself as a gun addict . . . he brought up his boys to shoot. The boy was in the Marines – taught to shoot again. . . . But the environmental history gets little notice. The mental and physiological fictions prevail. Whatever effect, if any, the tumour had, it did not *cause* the behaviour of taking an arsenal of guns and ammunition to a tower, barricading the doors, and shooting innocent people . . .
>
> (Skinner, 1980: 4)

Behaviour finds its source in 'controlling forces in the environment'. The tumour may have had some facilitating influence, but could never explain the *actual behaviour* of the murderer.

Emphatically, Skinner sought to develop an approach which was ***anti-dualist***. There is to be no gulf between the mind and the material world (see Kvale and Grenness, 1967; Valentine, 1992). We have already met the problem of dualism in looking at cognitive psychology, where the external world is somehow related to a quite distinct inner world of mental activity. In rejecting this, Skinner acknowledged the role of the person's genetic endowment but asserted that the major factors which explain behaviour are environmental ones. But 'environment' can be seen to include the body, and the usual connotation of the word as suggesting 'outer' in contrast to 'inner' must be set aside. We need to remember that environment refers to the regions inside the skin as well as the body's surroundings. Feelings and thoughts are behaviour for Skinner.

Skinner's non-dualist stance entails a rejection of the 'illusion of the double world' – the dualism of an outer, objective, physical world and an inner, subjective, psychological copy. Most psychologists retain this dualistic model, for instance in regarding conscious perception as an *interpretation* of physical sensations. This view is rejected by Skinner (1964), as we have seen in the critique section of the previous chapter.

Another feature of the dualistic view is a 'bifurcation of the public and private worlds'. Skinner points out that there is a widespread assumption that a person has a special kind of access to their own 'inner world' which is different from how they get knowledge of their surroundings (including other people). This idea is rejected by Skinner. He argues that we know the inner world through exactly the same processes that we know the outer world. The inner, 'private' world is not different in kind from the outer, 'public' world.

The key concepts of radical behaviourism

Operant conditioning: responses, stimuli, reinforcement

Take this example from the *Notebooks*. Skinner (1980: 162–163) reports noticing a man at an airport who was apparently doing his best to comfort his crying baby. At first Skinner was puzzled by the crying, but then the reason for it became plain. Each time the baby began to cry, the father responded 'by shifting the baby in his arms, jiggling it, or lifting it high in the air'. Unawares, the father was actually 'reinforcing' the crying.

In describing behaviour such as the baby's crying, a radical behaviourist begins with identifying a certain movement – an operant – a spontaneous response which operates on the environment. Maybe initially the baby spontaneously uttered an insignificant 'proto-cry'. Such an operant will occur, of course, at a particular time when it just so happens that certain stimulus conditions exist. In Skinner's example, the baby is in arms, in an otherwise meagre setting: the family is 'waiting'. Given such *stimulus conditions*, an operant may be succeeded by environmental circumstances which are contingent upon the operant – that is, they are consequences of it. The various activities of the father were contingent upon the baby's cry. Since the father's behaviour seems to have had the effect of strengthening the baby's operant behaviour, it is said to be *reinforcing*. When this kind of event has occurred – an operant has been strengthened by contingent reinforcement – then:

- The process is called operant *conditioning*. A class of responses has been affected by the consequences.
- The response is said to be under *stimulus control*. In circumstances of a similar kind (we cannot, without further evidence, guess what particular features of the baby's setting constituted stimuli for the crying) the behaviour will be evoked again.
- The condition of the environment following the response – contingent on it (in our case, the father's 'comforting'

actions) and which has had the effect of strengthening it – is said to *reinforce* the behaviour.

Shaping and chaining

Now, as I indicated, the initial state of the operant may not have been a full cry, but some insignificant vocalisation. But through *shaping*, the intensity of behaviour can be increased – the father's actions would elicit ever more 'enthusiastic' crying.

But more significantly, a complex piece of behaviour can be learned, starting off from a quite simple movement. For instance, initial clumsy attempts at using a computer mouse to click on an icon become precise and controlled over a period of time due to the reinforcing feedback from the screen – or better, the environment has acquired increasingly effective control over the behaviour entailed in moving the cursor using the mouse. And, having successfully stabilised a given operant, further behavioural elements can be *chained* onto it. The controlled movement of the mouse allows the conditioning of ever more subtle behaviours – so left-clicking on a particular point on the screen brings down a menu, which in turn can occasion a further extended sequence of behaviour.

It is important to see that reinforcement does not carry the same meaning as 'reward'. The only criterion for a contingent stimulus situation to be called a reinforcer is that it strengthens a response. There is no implication that it is 'felt' to be pleasurable (anxiously searching the horizon for an enemy is likely to be reinforced on occasions when enemies actually appear – but this is not pleasurable or rewarding in any usual sense). And no 'inner state' of the individual is referred to by the term 'reinforcement'.

Positive reinforcement, negative reinforcement and punishment

We can see now that a parent can reinforce, entirely unintentionally, precisely the behaviour that they intend to suppress. So the infant who is comforted on awakening and crying during the small hours of the night is likely to have that unfortunate behaviour reinforced. The main focus of attention of the advisers, to whom the poor, tired parents of infants with 'inappropriate sleep patterns' go for help, is not the infant but the parents themselves. They must be taught not to reinforce wakefulness – an exceedingly harrowing learning experience for them, but one which, if patiently endured, is virtually assured of success. The child will sleep.

So far, only positive reinforcement has been mentioned. But equally, the *removal* of an aversive stimulus situation may be reinforcing. This is negative reinforcement. Note, the contingent stimulus situation – the reinforcement – is not itself aversive, as the term might suggest. The negativity (confusingly) lies in the pre-existing situation, not in the reinforcement. In fact, for the parents in the recent example the crying of the wakeful infant in the night sets up precisely the kind of negative conditions which make it reinforcing *to them* to comfort the infant. And it is for this reason that their withdrawal of comfort is so difficult – they are themselves being deprived of negative reinforcement.

The situation in which an aversive situation is *contingent* on behaviour is usually called 'punishment', which is different from negative reinforcement. Skinner regards punishment as inefficient for learning. It is generally thought by laypeople that punishment will reduce the strength of the preceding behaviour. Even if it were observed that punishment does this, it is not clear precisely what is reinforced – notoriously, avoiding 'getting caught' is what punishment teaches the miscreant in some important situations. But in fact, evidence that punishment actually reduces response strength is lacking. Skinner seems to think that it simply 'drives the response underground', for the behaviour does remain within the person's repertoire. What is really required is that the response is *extinguished*. This does not call for some special kind of contingent stimulus, but simply that the response is not reinforced. In other words, ignoring untoward behaviour is often the appropriate technique, rather than punishment. Ideally, situations should not be set up so as to occasion undesirable behaviour.

Schedules of reinforcement: ratio, interval; fixed, variable

Skinner lays great stress on the frequency and manner of delivery of reinforcements. In the sort of experimental cage (called by others a 'Skinner Box') which dispenses food pellets at a frequency related to the rat's pressing of a lever, reinforcement of bar-pressing may be delivered in a number of ways. Food could appear after a certain number of presses (a 'ratio schedule'), or after a certain length of time (an 'interval schedule'). There are many such alternative *reinforcement schedules*. Both ratio and interval types may themselves be differentiated into fixed schedules and those in which the schedule varies in some way – maybe by increasing the length of time or number of presses before reinforcement is obtained. A great deal is known about the differences in experimental situations in the effectiveness of different reinforcement schedules (e.g. Ferster and Skinner, 1957).

Interpersonal relations and personal agency

Skinner did not see any need to distinguish between 'types' of reinforcer. For example, he asserted the equivalence of machine and person as a teacher (Skinner, 1980: 273). He would expect both to be as effective as each other, always assuming that, in both cases, the material is arranged in the order in which it is most effectively acquired.

Similarly, he was impatient with talk of 'interpersonal relations' (Skinner, 1980: 262) as if this labelled a distinct and mysterious realm of human contact. For him, behaviour between individuals simply entailed processes of reinforcement. Each person is part of the stimulus situation for the other, and possibly a source of reinforcement. But there is nothing distinctive about the 'meaning' of persons for each other.

Skinnerian thinking has had enormous influence on therapy. In a nutshell, the behaviour therapist determines precisely what the behaviour is which is felt to be undesirable, what the environmental situation is in which the unwanted behaviour occurs, and

***Box 4.1* Skinner on homosexuality**

In his informal *Notebooks*, Skinner speculates about homosexuality as being the consequence of an unavoidable lack of specificity in the genetically programmed receptiveness to sexually relevant stimuli:

> The argument that operant conditioning was 'the best thing that nature could do,' can be extended to sexual behavior.
>
> Heterosexual behavior is closely related to contingencies of survival, but nature could not be too specific. Strong personal affection, various forms of sexual stimulation, and possibly some built-in susceptibilities to particular visual forms and particular modes of stimulation – these are about the closest nature could come. But they produce homosexual and asexual behavior, which are not otherwise related to survival.
>
> (Skinner, 1980: 331)

On this account, gay and straight sexuality are equally *learned* orientations. Notoriously, behavioural approaches have in the past been used in order to attempt to re-orientate homosexuality.

what reinforcement sustains it. (The emphasis is on the current causes of behaviour, not the search for the biographical origin of the problem.) Then, having specified a preferred target behaviour to replace it, the conditions surrounding the behaviour – especially contingent reinforcement – are manipulated so that the desired target behaviour is conditioned. We have seen in the example of inappropriate sleep patterns in the infant how such work might be carried out in a simple case. In Box 4.1 I indicate some of the implications of Skinnerian behaviourism for homosexuality.

Not surprisingly, in view of Skinner's technical research on the process of operant conditioning, he is generally regarded as a *learning theorist*. It is, I believe, more profitable to view his work as having much wider impact than as a contribution to the study of a specific psychological function. Skinner is best understood as developing a very general psychological theory covering the totality of human activity. Central to it is a perspective on human nature as *inextricably part of the world's web of cause and effect. The way in which we are immersed in this structure is through the contingent reinforcement of behaviour*. As we saw in Skinner's own denial of his authorship of *Beyond Freedom and Dignity*, the individual makes no 'personal' contribution to the process.

Skinner's hermeneutics

Skinner's work often takes the form of a criticism and re-interpretation of psychological concepts. Intent on avoiding the dualism of the cognitive viewpoint, radical behaviourism is an interpretative and clarifying effort, a hermeneutics. A key text of this kind is *About Behaviourism* (1993).

Methodological behaviourists tended merely to argue that, as a requirement of scientific method, inner events should be regarded as non-existent. This decision having been made, problems of dualism do not arise because 'states of mind' are bypassed. Skinner, in contrast, meets dualism head on. He does not rule out private events, but he does question whether the usual psychological language is appropriate.

> Our increasing knowledge of the control exerted by the environment . . . makes it possible to interpret a wide range of mentalistic expressions. . . . Some can be 'translated into behaviour', others discarded as unnecessary or meaningless.
>
> (Skinner, 1993: 17)

It is to the environment that one looks for causes of behaviour – so Skinner criticises again the views of cognitive psychology as a dualism:

> Having moved the environment inside the head in the form of conscious experience and behaviour in the form of intention, will, and choice, and having stored the effects of contingencies of reinforcement as knowledge and rules, cognitive psychologists put them all together to compose an internal simulacrum of the organism, a kind of doppelganger, not unlike the classical homunculus . . . The mental apparatus studied by cognitive psychology is simply a rather crude version of contingencies of reinforcement and their effects.
> (Skinner, 1978: 109–110)

Skinner provides an interpretative method, then, a hermeneutics of the 'mental'. I will now outline some of his exercises in such hermeneutics.

Inner experience, feelings

For Skinner, although the body constitutes a 'private world', it is not different in kind from the rest of the cosmos. Inner sensations become known in the same way as outer stimuli. Generally other people label our behaviour as 'due to' inner stimuli, and in this way we become able to label such stimuli – thirst might be an example of this. But we know the 'small part of universe' within the skin *less well* than the public world, because the contingencies of reinforcement by which we learn are not so easily amenable to social manipulation. The events the reinforcement are 'about' are not available for others' scrutiny. Therefore, other people cannot easily label them for us and tell us what it is we are feeling.

In dealing with feelings, Skinner provides a number of interpretations which link them with events which can occur in schedules of reinforcement. For instance, 'The expression "frustrated expectations" refers specifically to a condition produced by the termination of accustomed reinforcement' (Skinner, 1993: 58). The *Notebooks* give a concrete example of this. Skinner discusses the situation in which a musical theme 'frustrates our expectations' (Skinner, 1980: 28). Given that Skinner regards perception as an active matter, a response, in listening to a piece of music one is not passively absorbing it but is actively engaged. Maybe the activity will involve covertly singing along with the theme. Maybe it will be noting the musical structure. In any case, when our expectations are frustrated, a well-learned response based on the way the music has gone so far turns out to be inappropriate. The composition deviates from the usual. The schedule of reinforcement has been interrupted. Of course such innovation could be delightful, but – delightful or frustrating – the feeling is a *response*. In general, he argues that feelings or states of mind are not themselves causes of behaviour but are by-products of the environmental contingencies which are the real cause.

It is worth noting here that recently behaviourists have set aside Skinner's assertion that 'inner processes' such as thinking and feeling are purely *responses* and can have no determinative effect on behaviour. This prejudice in any case goes against the major premise of his behaviourism that the individual is an inseparable part of the cosmos as a whole: if this is true, then thoughts and feelings must be involved in the flow of cause-and-effect, and they will produce consequences. This adjustment of Skinnerian theory has profound implications.

Perceiving

Skinner (1980: 256) reports a misperception due to the context. He had been using a small piece of paper as a coaster for his coffee cup, and, when he picked up the cup, the paper was lifted with the cup but then fell onto his hand. Skinner responded to the touch of the paper as if it were liquid – a drip from the cup – and moved to wipe it. The point of this instance is to indicate that perception is regarded by Skinner as an intrinsic part of the total structure of environment and behaviour. The response (wiping) is perceiving; the perceiving is therefore under the control of earlier stimulus situations (dripping coffee).

Skinner denies the need for the cognitive inner mechanism whereby raw stimuli are 'interpreted', and which leads to the achievement of perception. Instead, he insists that perception is the person's response to the current setting – integral to which is the relevant history of reinforcement (the setting now 'embodies' this history). 'We have no reason to say that he has stored information which he now retrieves in order to interpret the evidence of his senses' (Skinner, 1993: 78).

We will see this line of argument again in the context of 'memory'.

'Verbal behaviour'

Language has been a major area of contention between Skinnerians and their opponents, centring on the question of whether operant conditioning is an adequate account of how children acquire the rules of grammar (Skinner, 1957; Chomsky, 1959). The key thing for Skinner, however, was that verbal behaviour allows the person to become aware of their own contingencies of reinforcement – the causes of their actions. Thus 'rules' can be acquired which are to be regarded as *part of the stimulus environment* and therefore can come to play a part in the control of behaviour. Language enables the 'verbal community' to develop commands, advice, warnings, directions, instructions, rules, folklore, maxims, proverbs – all of which mean that behaviour comes under new categories of stimulus control.

When the verbal community begin to reinforce or (less effectively) punish behaviour on the basis of a label of 'good' or 'bad' and perhaps even lay down explicit rules, these can constitute part of the stimulus environment and assist both conformity to and enforcement of the norms. But, in line with his overall critique of dualistic cognitivism, Skinner emphasises that 'a person who learns these rules and behaves by explicitly following them still has not internalised them, even when he learns to control himself and thus to adjust even more effectively to the contingencies maintained by the group' (Skinner, 1993: 193). Why not? Skinner may seem to be simply objecting to the imagery of 'internalisation'. But this imagery implies that a person may be affected by the rules to such an extent that, whatever situation they are in, the rules will be 'with them', governing their behaviour. For Skinner, this is precisely the problem. To identify the rules as having become an inner property of the person's mental life distinguishes them unacceptably from the rest of the stimulus environment. Better, according to Skinner, to avoid even this dualism and regard the *environment* as having changed as a result of the acquisition of the rule.

Thinking

The principle that has just been underlined, that new verbal behaviour is to be regarded as part of the stimulus environment for a person, rather than an inherent property of the person themselves, becomes central to the understanding of Skinner's account of thinking.

> One scientist has said that 'there is excellent reason to believe that the whole world of chemistry is explicable in terms of electrons and the wave functions which describe their location. This is an enormous simplification of thought'. It certainly is an enormous simplification . . . but it is the simplification of verbal and practical behaviour rather than of thought. . . . [a] verbal environment has evolved in which obscure properties of nature are brought into the control of human behaviour.
>
> (Skinner, 1993: 106)

So the behaviour of the scientist, reinforced or extinguished as it may be by the actual contingencies of the world, may lead to the acquisition of new scientific findings. The findings themselves, labelled by the use of verbal or other symbols (themselves acquired by operant conditioning), may give rise to the statement of a scientific law (that is, some formulations are generated, and that which is reinforced by its match with reality is selected). But all this, though exceedingly high level behaviour, is describable in terms of reinforcing contingencies and stimulus situations. The scientist does not have any personal input to the process, and the scientific law is not properly described as internal to his or her mental life but is part of the environment.

This echoes the puzzling proposition with which this chapter started. It is possible to see that, in a certain sense, Skinner did not write *Beyond Freedom and Dignity*. However, the more-than-complex process whereby a myriad of environmental controls led to differentially reinforced behaviour which eventually culminated in the book, did lead to a change in the environment for Skinner. Skinner was the locus wherein the world produced the book, and the contents of the book then constituted part of his environment.

'Knowing how' versus 'knowing that'

We have seen how language enables contingencies of reinforcement to be constituted as part of the environment, therefore coming to control behaviour. Consider a person whose leisure activity was constrained by the fact that spirits gave them a headache. They might well find that the verbal formulation 'spirits give me a headache' affected their plans concerning alcohol-use such that spirits were avoided.

But how does Skinner cover this difference between the direct stimulus control of behaviour and the formulation of verbal 'knowledge' of this process of stimulus control. The question is the long-standing one of the distinction between 'knowing how' (or being able to do something) and 'knowing that' (or having a verbal account of how something is done). As Skinner (1993: 139) puts it, 'Knowledge which permits a person to describe contingencies is quite different from the knowledge identified with the shaping of behaviour. Neither form implies the other.'

He complains (1980: 211) that people who are expert in particular trades or professions are likely also to be assumed to know the psychology of their trade or profession. So 'Mathematicians are likely to describe how mathematicians think.' But knowing how to do mathematics and knowing about the nature of mathematicians' behaviour are different.

Remembering

Skinner notes that the 'cognitive metaphor' – which he rejects – likens remembering to the use of filing cabinets or notebooks. The idea that memory, especially long-term memory, is a matter of storage and retrieval is very well established in everyday discourse. Skinner dismisses all notions of memory as 'storing information in, and retrieving it from, one's head':

> The contingencies which affect an organism are not stored by it. They are never inside it; they simply change it. As a result, the organism behaves in special ways under special kinds of stimulus control. Future stimuli are effective if they resemble the stimuli which have been part of earlier contingencies. . . . Being reminded means being made more likely to respond . . .
>
> (Skinner, 1978: 109)

Rejection of dualism certainly means that the current state of the person-in-environment is an outcome of previous events, but these 'memories' are properties of the environment not the mind. There are many instances in Skinner's *Notebooks* of instances of remembering, all interpreted in environmental terms. He tells us of an occasion in which he seemed to be spontaneously recalling events of his childhood, but then notices his wife's movements in the kitchen. These noises are reminiscent of those caused years earlier by his parents' domestic activities, providing an environmental basis for the apparently spontaneous responses of 'remembering' (1980: 45). Similarly, his ability to play a saxophone after many years of neglect is also a function of the person-in-environment: The behaving was the remembering, and the stimulus situation that caused the behaviour was the saxophone in his hands ready to be played (ibid.: 313–314).

Self-knowledge and freedom

It is plain that, for Skinner, lack of freedom is axiomatic. One's behaviour is explicable in terms of controlling forces in the environment.

> The person who asserts his freedom by saying, 'I determine what I shall do next,' is speaking of freedom in or from a current situation: the I who thus seems to have an option is the product of a history from which it is not free and which in fact determines what it will now do.
>
> (Skinner, 1978: 168)

Beyond Freedom and Dignity is not his own work in the sense that he originated it or authored it in a fundamental sense. The person is a point at which a host of variables of the material world interact. The eventual behaviour is the product of reinforcing contingencies:

> We praise or blame as if people were responsible for their actions. They are right or wrong, admirable or despicable. But any resulting change is due to praise or blame, which is outside the individual. Praising and blaming recognise the individual 'as doer,' but there is no reason to say 'originator.'
>
> (Skinner, 1980: 306–307)

Yet Skinner does not regard it as an excuse to say 'that's just how I am' when confronted with one's own undesirable behaviour. It is true that Skinner would regard it as fruitless to try to change 'the self' (however this mental entity was construed). But he does indicate that, since one's behaviour is the outcome of the history of reinforcement, it is possible to engineer the situation so as to avoid circumstances which cause the unfortunate behaviour, or change the reinforcing contingencies. Unfreedom, it turns out, does not preclude behavioural change.

In so far as we are aware of our own behaviour and the contingencies to which we are subject, this is due to the application of linguistic labels. Self-knowledge is a verbal attempt to identify the controlling forces in the environment to which the individual is subject. And self-knowledge may well go astray due to un-behavioural notions of what one's action really is (that it is free; that it is due to certain personal characteristics of an inner kind, and so on).

Criticisms

Behaviourism is said to ***ignore consciousness, feelings and states of mind***. Skinner argues that radical behaviourism does not in fact ignore consciousness. By 'being conscious' Skinner means the individual *responds* perceptually or by feelings to those environmental stimuli for which there is a history of reinforcement. Additionally, a person becomes conscious in a different sense when others – a verbal community – arrange contingencies allowing that the person 'not only see an object but see that they are seeing it'. Here awareness is a social product.

There is a sense in which Skinner does give a behavioural account of consciousness, then. In my view, however, it neglects the real meaning of consciousness – which is the irreducible personal presence of the individual to his or her world. Skinner knows nothing of what we might term 'interiority'.

Similarly, Skinner has been criticised for assigning ***no real role to a self*** or sense of self. To this he unrepentantly pleads guilty – but denies any value to such notions.

> All selves are the product of genetic and environmental histories . . . There is no place in the scientific position for a self as true originator or initiator of action.
>
> (Skinner, 1993: 248)

This view may be countered by an opposing viewpoint which asserts that I am not the meeting point of numerous causal agencies which determine behaviour, but have an originary role in action. But more fundamental, in a way, than this assertion, contra

Skinner, that the person is an *agent*, is the recognition of the person as *subject*. This is the same as the point I have just made about the interiority of consciousness. There is something irreducible and inescapable about the nature of the human being as *having* or *owning* their subjective world. This fundamental fact is exceptionally difficult to label. Philosophers have sometimes attempted it, and in the next chapter we shall see the emphasis that Sartre places on this issue. The important point here is not whether Skinner was able to give a behaviouristic interpretation of knowing or the self, but rather that he did not at any point indicate that the human being has to be something (a self) for which the knowledge exists.

In Skinner, ***reinforcement*** is not to be taken as *emotional reward*; but nor can it be *feedback* in the sense of evidence to the individual that their intentions have been fulfilled. But the situations pointed to by these mentalistic notions are among those 'reinforcement' covers. It does seem that the concept covers a very large number of different kinds of consequences of behaviour that ought to be acknowledged and distinguished. Skinner's almost exclusive concern with operant conditioning as the one-and-only principle of human behaviour has been widely criticised. Chomsky's review of *Verbal Behaviour*, in which the features of language acquisition were paraded as evidence of unlearned tendencies in the child for abstracting *rules* for grammar, was particularly damaging to the Skinnerian position.

Skinner is adamant that an 'external' viewpoint on the person should be taken. The description of ***experience from the viewpoint of the experiencer*** – what may be called the phenomenological viewpoint – is avoided. Even if the environment increasingly takes on a character which includes the person's history of reinforcement, it is still objective. Yet the only approach which the researcher or therapist can make to the environment of an individual is to note their subjective responses, finding, for example, that the world outside the house is 'threatening' for this sufferer from 'agoraphobia'. In effect, the environment becomes saturated with personal meaning. It could be argued that the 'stimuli' affecting the person are no longer (if they ever were) a system of distinct 'variables', but a *lifeworld* made up of a web of meanings.

Summary

In essence, for Skinner human beings are distinguished from other entities in the universe only in that they are particularly susceptible to reinforcement, and for that reason their behaviour is especially affected by the environment.

- *Consciousness* means susceptibility to respond to stimuli because of prior reinforcement. It does not refer to the personal awareness of having experience. Neither is the conscious individual an agent (i.e. the active origin of their behaviour): a person is simply the place where many variables meet and cause behaviour.
- *Selfhood.* Other people provide reinforcing contingencies whereby selfhood (as self-description) arises. But the idea of selfhood as involving 'interiority' – oneself as the personal subject of experience – is not acknowledged by Skinner.
- *The body* is significant for Skinner, in that it is the individual as a physical entity which, as part of the physical world, is open to environmental control through contingencies of reinforcement. But the body should not be seen as marking off a distinction between the 'inner' and 'outer' world.
- *Other people.* In the form of the 'verbal community' other people are a determinant of action. Other people, however, are not special in the sense of having a distinct and unparalleled significance for the person. Other stimuli and reinforcers are of equivalent status.
- *The physical world.* The world is the totality of stimuli which control behaviour. Behaviour is totally explicable in terms of its causal action. But my particular world is also unique in that only I have been subjected to precisely my set of contingencies of reinforcement.

Further reading

The classic source is B.F. Skinner's (1953) *Science and Human Behaviour*, New York: The Free Press. A late defence of his viewpoint is provided in Skinner, B.F. (1993) *About Behaviourism,* London: Penguin.

Kvale, S. and Grenness, C.E. (1967) 'Skinner and Sartre: Towards a radical phenomenology of behaviour?', *Review of Existential Psychology and Psychiatry*, 7, 128–148, and Blackman, D.E. (1991) 'B.F. Skinner and G.H. Mead: On biological science and social science', *Journal of the Experimental Analysis of Behavior*, 55, 251–265, both compare Skinner to other authors – finding surprising areas of concordance.

Richelle, M.N. (1993) *B.F. Skinner: A Reappraisal*, Hove: Erlbaum, provides a sympathetic – and scholarly – account.

Chapter 5

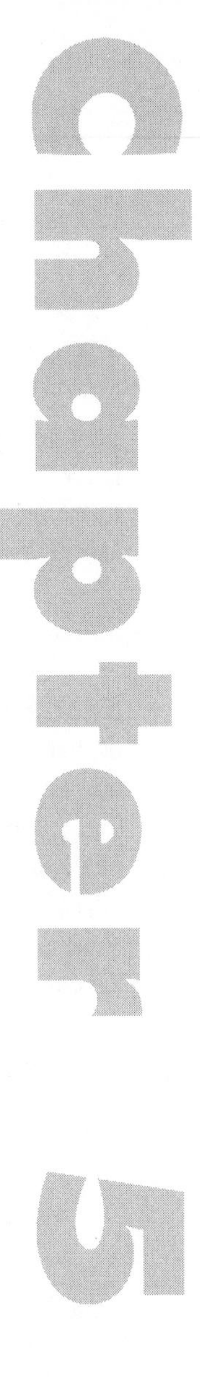

The individual consciousness: anxiously free in a meaningless world

AS I POINTED OUT IN THE INTRODUCTION, it is right in a book about the diversity of views concerning human nature to consider writers outside, or even antagonistic to, the discipline of psychology. The horizon of members of the psychological guild is likely to have limitations which only an outsider will challenge. Existentialism, the philosophy with which Jean-Paul Sartre (1905–1980) is identified, does attack the mainstream of the discipline (though it is also true that it has had a major influence on humanistic psychology).

The leading existentialist dismissed psychology in the following words. 'Quite frankly, I do not believe in the existence of psychology. I have not done it and I do not believe it exists' (see Schilpp, 1981: 38). What can Sartre have understood psychology to be, if it led him to distance himself so strongly from it? After all, he had written on imagination (1972) and emotion (1962) – matters central to psychology – and his major work, *Being and Nothingness* (1958) has a chapter entitled 'Existential Psychoanalysis'.

Psychology often claims to have the aim of explaining and predicting human actions. For Sartre, this aim is forlorn and the thinking on which it is based is a falsehood. As fellow existentialist Merleau-Ponty (1962: viii), emphasised, our experience and action is not the outcome of some set of variables, interacting with each other in conformity with certain natural laws. The sense we make of the world is not explicable in terms of the psychologist's knowledge, however detailed, of such things as our environmental circumstances or our biological constitution. Existentialists challenge the determinism of the majority of psychologists. We are 'condemned to freedom', and it is important in this book that arguments against deterministic psychology should be heard.

What Sartre was trying to do

To base his work on ***phenomenology***. Sartre, following the founder of phenomenology, Edmund Husserl (1859–1938), insisted that the conceptual basis of a science must be secured in experience. This is a 'return to the things themselves'. Husserl sought a description of the essence of a particular 'phenomenon' – the thing purely as given in experience – as the basis for any further research activity. For instance, the study of fear must be founded in the description of the experience of fear (though such work might discover that there is no typical mode of fear, there could be several). No mere definition of fear would do, it had to be the detailed description of fear. As Merleau-Ponty put it, personal experience is regarded by phenomenologists as primary. Scientific accounts are secondary elaborations of it:

> All my knowledge of the world, even my scientific knowledge, is gained from my own particular point of view, or from some experience of the world without which the symbols of science would be meaningless.
>
> To return to things themselves is to return to that world which precedes knowledge, of which knowledge always *speaks*, and in relation to which every scientific schematisation is an abstract and derivative sign-language, as is geography in relation to the countryside in which we have learnt beforehand what a forest, a prairie or a river is.
>
> (Merleau-Ponty, 1962: viii, ix)

To focus on the description of 'human reality', distinguishing firmly between ***consciousness and the objects of consciousness***. In Sartre's view, the separation of consciousness itself from anything that one can be conscious of is a fundamental finding of phenomenology. It is on this distinction that the rest of his analysis rests. Consciousness is understood to be open to content, but not to have any intrinsic characteristics of its own.

To carry through the implications of the view that, since the individual person is a consciousness, ***the individual has no***

'essence'. In the division between consciousness/objects of consciousness, personal attributes are wholly on the side of the object and this meant for Sartre that the person has no 'dyed-in' features. Plainly this is a major challenge to the very many psychological theories which provide characterisations of types of individuals. The term 'existentialism' itself refers to this view that the person is without essential characteristics and ought primarily to be thought of as simply *an existent*.

For Sartre, the lack of essence of an individual was a particularly valuable finding (if this it was) because it was the foundation for ***human freedom***. Though Sartre knew very well that we are fettered by economics, power, etc., he understood the person to be, nevertheless, a free constructor of the meaning of the situation. Such construing is always open to change.

To investigate the ***ambiguity of personal relationships***. The meeting of a free individual with another, equally free, is extremely fraught in Sartre's view. The other person necessarily construes us – endows us with characteristics – and this 'objectification' is an implicit constraint on our freedom. At the same time we are objectifying them. Interpersonal relations are inevitably conflictual.

To provide a method for the analysis of the individual. Such an ***existential analysis*** must arrive at a description of the person in terms of the choice he or she has made of the kind of person to be within their actual situation. Sartre's approach to the description of a person is, at one and the same time, a way of doing biographical writing, and a kind of individual, existential psychoanalysis.

An outline of Sartre's existentialism

I shall treat each of the five aspects of Sartre's approach to human nature in turn: phenomenology, consciousness versus objects of consciousness, the self and the essenceless of the individual, interpersonal relations, and existential psychoanalysis.

Phenomenological methodology

Some psychologists have been slapdash in their application of the term 'phenomenology'. Any theoretical position or method of qualitative research that gives a place to the individual's point of view (e.g. Kelly's theory, which is plainly cognitive) can get categorised as 'phenomenological'. The characteristics of phenomenological research listed in Box 5.1 – and this is only an indication of the approach – show that there is considerably more to phenomenological research than a focus on individual experience.

Orthodox experimental psychology is 'positivistic' (see Chapter 3), the key thing being the idea that there is an underlying unequivocal reality, consisting of a web of relationships among specifiable variables, and scientific theories are testable models of that reality. In contrast, phenomenologically based investigation is a descriptive study of selected phenomena of the lifeworld of individuals.

Elements of the lifeworld are not variables (which are separate and distinct) because, in lived experience, the meaning of one element is dependent on that of the others. Take age, for instance. For positivism, an individual's age is the definite value of a variable. No doubt, in a model of some psychological process, age will interact with other variables, but its numerical value is not affected. A person's age as a meaning, perceived by them in the context of their lifeworld, is very different. Here 'fifty-two' is intrinsically changed by the context in which it becomes salient. The very meaning is altered. So the lifeworld is a kind of web of interrelated elements in which the meaning of each depends on the rest. Thus phenomenology recognises that the configuration of meanings surrounding 'daffodil' will be different for a market gardener pressed by hard economic conditions and for a poet who wanders unexpectedly across a host of them. Daffodils have a different place in these two lifeworlds.

Now, this takes us close to the phenomenological method which Sartre used. In *Being and Nothingness*, Sartre uses phenomenological description to tease out the most general principles of lived experience.

Box 5.1 **Phenomenologically based psychological research**

- Turns for its subject-matter to the ***experience of the individual research participant.*** No presupposition is made that this experience relates to one unequivocal, real, shared world.
- The experience sought is not introspective in the sense of requiring the research participant to report on their 'mental processes', but rather tries to develop a ***description*** of aspects of their experienced ***lifeworld*** – their actual situation as it appears to them (including emotional meanings, etc.).
- The features of the lifeworld are not variables, but ***meanings***. That is, each part of the description has intrinsic links with each other part; the meaning of one element is only understandable in relation to the situation as a whole.
- To achieve a description of the research participant's lifeworld, the researcher must adopt a particular self-discipline. Certain kinds of presupposition must be set aside or ***bracketed***: (a) *Science*, in the sense of a body of 'known facts', must be bracketed in order to avoid inadvertently importing theories and findings which would distort the description of the lifeworld. (b) The usual idea of *validity* must be set aside. Since the research participant's experience is the topic of research, the researcher is debarred from querying the validity of the lifeworld. It *is* as it appears to them to be (e.g. Husserl, 1970: 240).

Consciousness and the objects of consciousness

Sartre's main concern was to clarify the most fundamental features of lived experience. The basic notion which comes out of descriptions of psychological phenomena is *intentionality*. Every mental act is intentional in that it is *of something*. This sense of intentionality, which is not to be confused with other senses of the word such as purposefulness, focuses on the finding that all perceiving, or feeling, or remembering, etc., has content.

For Sartre consciousness is one thing, and the phenomena of which we are conscious are of a different order of reality. There are two ontologically distinct kinds of things: *objects of consciousness* and *consciousness*. Sartre wants to make us graphically aware of a gap between things and our consciousness of things. Sartre is (to this extent) a dualistic thinker. But at the same time dualism is overcome through the recognition (a) that there is no object of consciousness devoid of human meaning, and (b) consciousness 'in the abstract' is never found, it is always *of something*.

- **Objects**, things, experiences, concepts – anything perceptible or conceivable by consciousness. He terms these 'beings in themselves' (*êtres-en-soi*). In the sense introduced earlier, they are 'intentional objects'. The objects of which we are aware are never known 'objectively'. We are conscious of them in their subjective meaning for us, and the meaning is not fixed; we could view the object differently. Sartre says, then, that we are 'condemned to freedom'. Merleau-Ponty prefers the formulation, 'condemned to meaning'. We are meaning-attributing consciousnesses.
- **Consciousness**. This is not an object. It is never perceived, rather it is what 'does' the perceiving, feeling, remembering and conceiving. Consciousness is intentional, always being of something. We can of course form a concept of consciousness, but this is not the same as having access to pure consciousness itself. Not characterisable itself, it is, as Sartre says, *nothingness*. But, in being conscious, one is, so to speak, aware of being aware. In this sense there is a kind of reflexivity about consciousness, which Sartre registers in labelling it 'being for itself' (*être-pour-soi*).

In a claim that had profound implications for Sartre's view of human nature, he argues that for consciousness to be intentional – for it to be able to construe objects freely – *the individual must not themselves have intrinsic, essential characteristics*. These would be limitations on the capacity of consciousness to construct meaning creatively. Consciousness is (in the word in the title of his major work) nothingness, no-thing-ness. The conscious individual has no inherent characteristics, and this opens up consciousness to possibilities – setting aside, for example, present constructions of reality in favour of what might be. This nothingness, and the creativity it allows, is part of what Sartre means by freedom.

Selfhood and the individual's lack of essential characteristics

As a consciousness, the individual person has no 'essence'. What does it imply for Sartre's view of human nature that consciousness must not be thought of as having intrinsic characteristics? Among other things, it means that the self – in the sense of the set of a person's attributed characteristics – is not part of consciousness but is an object for consciousness. This point was the central message of one of Sartre's (1957) earliest philosophical publications. The viewpoint is echoed by Merleau-Ponty (1962: xi): 'There is no inner man, man is in the world, and only in the world does he know himself.'

Incidentally, Merleau-Ponty's gendered language (uncontroversial at the time) brings us up short today. But this enables a valuable point about the existentialist understanding of self and consciousness to be made tellingly. For gender would be an aspect of self – the intentional object – and not at all an intrinsic feature of consciousness. Consciousness as such is not gendered, nor can it be categorised in terms of any other 'variable'. This is by no means to gainsay the existential impact of those social conditions which render gender salient and of which Sartre's lifelong co-worker Simone de Beauvoir wrote profoundly in *The Second Sex* (1988). Rather, it reinforces the feminist case.

The idea that self is not intrinsic to consciousness is made clearer if one considers the experience of being absorbed in a task that requires concentration. In that immediate experience, there is no awareness of one's 'personality': one is entirely 'out there' in performing the task. It is possible, of course, at any time, to come to oneself and reflect on the situation and one's involvement in it. But Sartre's point is that this is a separate act of reflection. In actually being absorbed in the task there is no thematic awareness of self.

Why cannot individual consciousness be regarded as a self? We have seen that consciousness, in being aware of some 'intentional' object (i.e. having something in mind) is aware (a) of that thing and (b) of itself simply as the 'awareness'. But the reflexivity of (b) is nothing to do with the social, biological, biographical self. And as we have seen, it is important for Sartre's approach that consciousness should be empty of any of the special characteristics we attribute to selves. These would affect the freedom of consciousness to construe the world.

Self is a 'useless passion'

So, consciousness and intentional objects are two distinct forms of being. To be both consciousness and solidly characterisable is impossible. Amalgamation into the category *pour-et-en-soi* cannot be. Self is not 'wired into' consciousness, and as consciousnesses we are never characterisable as purely and simply such-and-such a 'type'. There is always a certain freedom to construct one's own meaning-interpretation of oneself and the situation, in or out of jail.

For existentialists, it is a logical error to regard a person as intrinsically having such-and-such a nature. A term like 'cowardly' is rightly used if it is understood to be a just summary statement for a history of actions. But it is wrongly used if it is supposed to refer to an intrinsic personal characteristic. The next situation that arises will require a fresh choice of action, a new construction of self. This is even the case when one understands that there are factual aspects of the situation which cannot be gainsaid (see Box 5.2 for the case of homosexuality).

Sartre regards the no-thing-ness, the lack of an inherent self, of consciousness as the major motivating feature of human beings. For its lack of solidity, objectness and selfhood is an abiding *anxiety* of the conscious being: in fact, this is the definitive meaning of anxiety for Sartre. Sartre claims that the conscious individual is (without any special reflection) appalled at its own

***Box 5.2* Simone de Beauvoir on homosexuality**

In *The Second Sex* (1988 translation of 1949 original), Simone de Beauvoir summarises the existentialist approach to homosexuality – in this case, lesbianism, but the argument is interchangeable. This passage also elucidates the approach of de Beauvoir, Sartre and their ilk to all those characteristics which we take to be facts about ourselves. We still have to choose how to *live* them, maybe by denying them.

> The truth is that homosexuality is no more a perversion deliberately entered into than it is a curse of fate. It is an attitude *chosen in a certain situation* – that is, at once motivated and freely adopted. No one of the factors that mark the subject in connection with this choice – physiological conditions, psychological history, social circumstances – is the determining element, though they all contribute to its explanation. It is one way among others, in which woman solves the problems posed by her condition in general, by her erotic situation in particular. Like all human behaviour, homosexuality leads to make-believe, disequilibrium, frustration, lies, or, on the contrary, it becomes the source of rewarding experience, in accordance with the manner of expression in actual living – whether in bad faith, laziness and falsity, or in lucidity, generosity, and freedom.
>
> (de Beauvoir, 1988: 444)

nothingness; there is a constant tinge of anguish at the fact of the negativity and freedom of consciousness. We have no guidelines for the meanings we impose on ourselves and the situation.

How do we allay the anxiety? By denying our no-thing-ness. By pretending objectness. That is, by taking on a self as if it were intrinsic rather than chosen. 'Man is a useless passion', Sartre says, in commentary on our vain attempt to become *pour-et-en-soi*. The individual pretends to be a character, adopts determinate characteristics. Existential psychoanalysis, we shall see, aims to uncover a person's particular way of denying freedom and nothingness.

Bad faith

The anxiety of consciousness in the face of its nothingness is allayed by bad faith – the identification of consciousness with the characterful self. A logical impossibility, we are led to understand. Yet this attempt at self-objectification is said to be the goal which everyone pursues. To objectify oneself is bad faith. The term is also used to refer to the refusal of responsibility for choices one has made – which are always made in freedom according to Sartre.

- *Bad faith as the identification of oneself with a role.* Sartre describes (1958: 59) the café waiter who identifies so much with the role that he cannot be imagined – or imagine himself – as anything but a waiter. The person is avoiding confrontation with his actual freedom and nothingness by adopting the role as if this made him into an object.
- *Bad faith as refusal to take responsibility for choice.* The woman whose companion for the evening has begun to hold her hand, may pretend ignorance that this has happened and that it calls for a choice of response (Sartre, 1958: 55). Here the bad faith is in refusing responsibility for a choice by denying having made it. To deny responsibility for the meanings inevitably imposed on the situation is bad faith. In the example, Sartre is making it clear that to passively allow one's hand to be held is actually a choice and is not an escape from freedom.
- *Bad faith as unreflective acceptance of social attributions.* The novel *Nausea* (Sartre, 1965), provides a telling example of bad faith. Having inspected the picture gallery with its portraits of the great and good of the town ('Bouville'), the character Roquentin turns to address the worthies' portraits: 'Farewell, you beautiful lilies, elegant in your little painted

sanctuaries, farewell, you beautiful lilies, our pride and raison d'être, farewell, you Bastards' (ibid.: 138).

Why such violent language? Sartre is accusing the smug, the bourgeois (less a class here than an attitude) of bad faith. They know themselves to be safe, at home, and their values to be correct. They have the 'spirit of Seriousness' (Sartre, 1958: 626) which is a version of bad faith. It involves taking one's social attributes, especially one's values, seriously as 'wired in' rather than chosen. Sartre opposes this with *lightness* (which he does not expand on, but which seems to me a most important ethical notion).

Interpersonal relations

A basic difficulty in realising freedom consists in the conflicts that are implicit in intersubjectivity. We are always subject to the risk of objectification in the eyes of other people. Called 'the Look', the gaze of the other is a deprivation of spontaneity, of freedom. A description (Sartre, 1958: 255) demonstrates the objectifying nature of the Look. I am taking a stroll in the park. The empty scene is spread out before my awareness, and it is laid out with *me* as the source of its perspective, relative distances, etc. Then, suddenly, I realise that there is someone sitting on that bench, and, in that moment, the meaning of the scene is changed: it is no longer merely for myself, but is a scene for the other, and I am part of that scene as far as that other person is concerned – an object of her awareness.

The awareness of one's objectness for others (a) allows the possibility of reflective thinking (notably consciousness of self); (b) allows the possibility of living in bad faith in line with the objectification of others, and (c) leads to conflict in interpersonal relations.

- *Being-for-others and reflective consciousness.* Self-awareness has a social origin; it arises in the Look of the other – we become the focus of our own awareness when we recognise that others have a point of view in which we figure as objects. This gives us the possibility of self-reflection.

- *Freedom, bad faith, and objectification by others.* We may choose in bad faith to live out the roles or characteristics ascribed to us by others, pretending that they are essential to us. Escape from bad faith, if possible, would be an espousal of anxious freedom – in fact the choice of bad faith seems so inevitable that Fell (1970) has even argued that there is a deterministic theory of motivation hidden in Sartre's view of the desire to escape from anxious freedom.

Conflict in interpersonal relations

In *In Camera* (1946), the character Garcin voices Sartre's own thought: 'Hell is other people.' I am an object for them, and this construction robs me of my status as a consciousness; at the same time I am engaged in the objectification of them. An irreconcilable conflict is intrinsic to interpersonal relations.

In a relationship with another person, there are two consciousnesses, free and spontaneous, but each perceiving the other as object, and seeing themselves as objectified. Conflict is the central meaning of being-for-others. Sartre expands on intimate interpersonal relations at length in *Being and Nothingness*. The main claim is that love entails the desire to possess the other person – but as a freedom. The attempted solution, Sartre says, is to attempt to become the 'whole world' for the other person so that they freely enter into one's possession.

In *sadism*, the attempt is made to dominate and objectify the other. But this fails since the loved object is a consciousness, and there is always residual freedom on their part. This cannot be enslaved. In *masochism*, the attempt is made through voluntarily becoming an object for the other, concealing freedom in order to be the desirable thing for the other. The ideal might seem to be a dual sadism/masochism, with one partner taking a submissive and the other a dominating attitude. But this fails even as it succeeds because what was in view was the capturing of a freedom, which now, in the masochist, voluntarily goes into hiding.

Even at this stage it is right to mention that Sartre's view of human relationships as a battle of mutual objectification in the context of two distinct freedoms has been sharply criticised. Sartre seems to have worked on the purely abstract level, drawing out the implications of his consciousness/object distinction without going back to the actual phenomena of interpersonal relations. If he had done so, as Merleau-Ponty (1962: 361) points out, he would have found that, although the kinds of relationships he describes (and which Scheler [1954] had earlier discussed under the headings idiopathic and heteropathic identification) certainly do exist, they only do so within a mood of mutual scrutiny. Much interaction is carried out within a taken-for-granted framework of trust, in which participants are able to set aside concern with objectification and get on with their joint activities.

Existential psychoanalysis

In the light of his refusal of characteristics to consciousness, Sartre's antagonism to the psychology of personality, especially psychoanalysis, is understandable. For Sartre, human reality is to be viewed in terms of the 'ends it pursues'. A person's aims should be sought in order to understand them, and the focus of interpretation should be on the reasons they have for their actions rather than looking for blind causes. For Sartre, a reason for an action specifies what in my world I want to change as a result of my action. The 'objective state of affairs' only leads to an action if it is constituted as a reason by consciousness. This entails the imaginative construction of the situation as currently entailing a *lack* which I can try to remedy. This account underlines responsibility for actions. 'Factual' things – my biography, personal biology, place in society – provide a situation in which I can apprehend a lack that gives a reason for action. I am responsible for the interpreted facts, the definition of the situation.

Original project

Now notwithstanding spontaneity and freedom, *a person's history of choices is not chaotic*. How can this be? Sartre has dismissed the very idea of a psychology of personality that would account for the person's 'choices' as the lawful outcome of certain innate or learned characteristics. Rather, his explanation of the non-chaotic nature of a person's behaviour is that, in anxiety in the face of the 'vacuum that consciousness is', one chooses a kind of person to be. Existential psychoanalysis investigates the biography of a person in order to uncover the pervading style of choices. This style reveals the meaning of the whole life. It is the 'original project'.

It is in Sartre's biographies that one sees existential psychoanalysis at work. For instance, in *Baudelaire* (Sartre, 1949) we see the formation of the original project of this poet in the disruption of his almost symbiotic relationship with his mother:

> Baudelaire was six when his father died. He worshipped his mother and was fascinated by her. He was surrounded by every care and comfort; he did not yet realise that he existed as a separate person, but felt that he was united body and soul to his mother in a primitive mystical relationship. . . . The mother was an idol, the child *consecrated* by her affection for him. Far from feeling that his existence was vague, aimless, superfluous, he thought of himself as a *son by divine right* . . .
>
> In November 1828 the mother whom he worshipped remarried. Baudelaire was sent to boarding school . . . His mother's second marriage was the one event in his life which he just could not accept. . . . 'When one has a son like me . . . one doesn't remarry.'
>
> The sudden break and the grief it caused forced him into a personal existence without any warning or preparation. One moment he was still enveloped in the communal religious life of his mother and himself; the next, life had gone out like a tide leaving him high and dry. The justification for his existence had disappeared; he made the mortifying discovery that he was a single person, that his life had been given him for nothing. . . . When later on he thought of this moment, he wrote in *Mon coeur mis à nu*:

> 'Sense of solitude from childhood. In spite of the family – and above all when surrounded by children of my own age – I had a sense of being destined to eternal solitude.'
>
> He already thought of his isolation as a destiny. That meant that he did not accept it passively. . . . This brings us to the point at which Baudelaire chose the sort of person he would be. He felt and was determined to feel that he was unique.
>
> (Sartre, 1949: 16–18)

So Sartre's existential psychoanalysis of Baudelaire uncovers a pervasive *project* – to be unique. Perhaps this example is sufficient to give a flavour of the sort of quasi-psychological work which Sartre's viewpoint permits. The aim is to discover the theme of the choices a person has made.

Sartre and humanistic psychology

I mentioned that existentialism has had a significant impact on humanistic psychology. Yet the nature of that impact is not clear-cut. The detailed analyses of Sartre have not entered into humanistic psychology generally. The aspect of existentialist thinking which is most clearly recognisable is an emphasis on the primacy of personal viewpoint. But this is not carried through to the extent that the conceptual framework of humanistic psychology is grounded in universal categories of experience – phenomenology in its strict sense is not employed. A general assumption of human freedom is also adopted by humanistic psychologists, certainly to the extent that a person is understood to be capable of personal change. But here again, humanistic psychologists do not adopt the more rigorous – or extreme – position of existentialism in viewing the nothingness of consciousness and the characterlessness of the individual as a necessary correlate of human freedom. In some formulations of humanistic psychology we find something more like *essentialism* than existentialism, in which it is held that each person has a kind of innate selfhood which, with a certain attitude towards oneself, can be developed. For Rogers, for instance, the typical client 'in the therapeutic relationship, with its freedom from threat and freedom of choice' experiences a movement in which he can:

> permit himself freely to be the changing, fluid process which he is. He moves also toward a friendly openness to what is going on within him – learning to listen sensitively to himself. . . . It means that as he moves toward acceptance of the 'is-ness' of himself he accepts others increasingly in the same listening, understanding way.
>
> (Rogers, 1967: 181)

This characteristic passage indicates the actual gulf between Sartrean existentialism and humanistic psychology. And of course, for all his talk of 'existential psychoanalysis', Sartre was not himself putting forward a therapy. Indeed, Roger's client-centred and non-directive approach to therapy presupposes the possibility of an unthreatening relationship of mutual understanding which Sartre would regard as naïve in the face of the clash of freedoms and mutual objectification of actual human relationships.

Criticisms

Sartre's theory is individualistic. The method of phenomenological description does entail a starting point in individual experience. In Sartre, the tendency to see interpersonal relations as a threat is another indication of individualism.

Sartre's version of existentialism is ***irrationalist and pessimistic.*** People have no guidelines for ethical action, no hope of attaining a solid and anxiety-free personhood/personality, and their choices are futile. A counter-claim might be to argue that, in existentialism, choices are genuine ones – not dictated by determinants or clear-cut rules. For choices to be fully moral, *decisions must be made freely*. It is in this spirit that Sartre opposes the acceptance-in-bulk of any ideology:

> I'd like to explain my opinion of the Communists I've met, under the circumstances in which I've met them. They smiled, they talked, they replied to the questions I asked them, but in fact it was not they who were replying. 'They' vanished and became characters whose principles one knew and who gave the answer *L'Humanité* would have given in the name of these principles.
>
> (Sartre, in de Beauvoir, 1984: 403)

Consciousness – when does it occur, and is it distinct from bodily functioning? It is essential to consciousness that it is inalienably self-aware. Part-and-parcel of being conscious of something is to be intrinsically aware of being conscious. Recently, Sartre's view of consciousness has been subjected to some major criticism in the light of the so-called 'problem of the long-distance truck-driver' (Armstrong, 1981). This refers to the common experience of having driven for a distance with one's 'mind on other things' and then coming to a realisation that the road has been followed without mishap, but one has not been aware of it at all.

Presumably one's body of itself is intentional in the phenomenological sense. There is a vast range of activities – habitual ones, for instance – on which the full spotlight of consciousness does not need to be turned, yet they are carried out with real attunement to varying features of the external world. The literature of perception reports other, less everyday, occurrences of successful judgements without awareness, such as 'blindsight' (see, for example, Weiskrantz, 1988).

Surely the driver's successful driving despite lacking thematic awareness of the road means that Sartre's unitary notion of consciousness is incorrect. Do we say that not all consciousness is *pour-soi*? Certainly the driver's skilful work has the hallmarks of intentionality: the events on the road are non-consciously 'understood' as meaningful and adjustments made. Yet this intentionality is not self-aware. Wider (1997) provides a detailed analysis of this issue. If consciousness loses its character of being intrinsically self-aware, then much of the rest of Sartre's work (freedom and responsibility – bad faith and original project) is at hazard.

An over-emphasis on freedom. Of course, the freedom Sartre discussed was not freedom of action (which very much depends on the factual conditions of the world) but the intrinsic freedom of consciousness to construe. But, just as we seem to have levels of appropriate attunement to our surroundings which are not fully open to awareness, so our active construing and re-construing of our situation, which constitutes freedom in Sartre's sense, may be more limited in practice than he assumes.

A related criticism is of Sartre's ***non-determinism***. The central value given to freedom is the major source of the criticisms which psychologists would be expected to lodge against Sartre's version of existentialism. Determinism is presupposed by psychologists generally as a necessary assumption for scientific work. Yet the voluntarism of Sartre's theory rules out the predictability of human action. To some extent, this is mitigated by the notion of 'original choice' which does reintroduce an element of continuity in individual personality which, while not determined in the strict sense, nevertheless provides predictability.

Dualism and phenomenology. We have passed without comment over the centrality of the distinction between consciousness and its intentional objects, but many existential phenomenologists have regarded it as nonsense to separate the two (e.g. Luijpen, 1966). Consciousness as such can never be described in isolation, but only as a consciousness of something, an intentionality.

Summary

- *Consciousness*. This is the central fact of human nature in Sartre's account, and has a lengthy list of implications for his notions of freedom, selfhood, original choice, the meaning of the other, and the nature of personal responsibility.
- *Selfhood* is not intrinsic to consciousness. One espouses selfhood in escaping from the rootlessness of consciousness. This

gives an ambiguity to the way in which self is constructed in the face of other people. They constrain and label us, but also provide the means by which one knows oneself.

- *The body* is an object for consciousness. Therefore, how it is construed is an achievement of freedom.
- *Other people*. In the same way as there is ambiguity about the self, there is ambiguity about other people. Their Look is objectifying of one; it classifies one and therefore limits one's spontaneity. Others are imperialists, and the more intimate the relationship, the more this is so. Yet it is in relationship with others that reflective consciousness comes to be.
- *The physical world*. For Sartre the world is meaningless and absurd, but the raw material for human meaning-interpretation. Consciousness has not got a fixed repertoire of meanings that it fixes on things. It is the spontaneous act of consciousness to give meaning. Yet the meaning a person chooses can be understood.

Further reading

Jean-Paul Sartre's key existentialist work is *Being and Nothingness* (New York: Philosophical Library, 1958). It cannot be said to be straightforward for the reader. His novel *Nausea* (London: Penguin, 1965) embodies the same outlook and is, in a certain sense, more enjoyable. Iris Murdoch's *Sartre* (London: Collins, 1967) is an exposition and commentary drawing on both his philosophical and literary work. A. Danto, *Sartre* (2nd edn: London: Collins, 1991), takes the author's main conceptual analyses and expounds them sympathetically and readably.

The classic paper by Kvale and Grenness (1967), mentioned at the end of the previous chapter, is well worth seeking out. My own 'L'Enfer, c'est les autres: Goffman's Sartrism', *Human Studies*, 8, 97–168 (1985), similarly attempts to clarify the thought of two important authors by allowing each to interpret the meaning of the other.

Chapter 6

Social being: interacting, and presenting oneself as a person

chapter 6

IN THIS CHAPTER I BEGIN WITH TWO WRITERS, G.H. Mead (1863–1931) and Erving Goffman (1922–1982), who are generally classified as *symbolic interactionists*. The label must be viewed warily, but there is no doubt about the similarity of approach of these two authors. The symbolic interactionist view of human nature is radically social. Mead (1934: 186) tells us, 'What I want particularly to emphasise is the temporal and logical pre-existence of the social process to the self-conscious individual that arises within it.' Mind and self are products of social interaction. Goffman would agree.

The approach of Mead and Goffman has so much in common with *discourse analysis* and related recent tendencies within social psychology (Potter and Wetherell, 1987; Hollway, 1989; Burman and Parker, 1993; Harré and Gillett, 1994) that it is not misleading to present them all together.

George Herbert Mead

In the early 1900s it went without comment for an American philosopher to offer courses in social psychology to students with sociological interests. This Mead did, and strongly influenced maybe three generations of sociologists through that teaching. His written output was, in contrast, slim, and the books that bear his name are in fact posthumously edited. The volume that is most significant for our purposes, *Mind, Self and Society* (Mead, 1934), tends to be repetitive and inconsistent. His thought is best approached through secondary sources.

What Mead was trying to do

Mead was a ***pragmatist*** philosopher. This school has a number of characteristics that are important for understanding his views. It involves *consequentialism*. That is, pragmatism regards formal thinking as a technology, aimed at producing tangible results; the meaning of concepts lies in their consequences (Baldwin, 1986). Beliefs are not to be held simply because they are in keeping with some general outlook, but are required to show their valuable consequences. Pragmatism also holds that the tools of thought, scientific and other knowledge, are always *tentative* – partly because conceptions of the world continually develop, but also because new phenomena emerge to be explained.

Mead was also an ***anti-dualist: mind is part of the natural world.*** The discussion of mental events must be made compatible with the way events in the natural world are discussed. For example, Mead's claim that mind comes about through the internalisation of early communication between infant and caregiver enabled him to construct a unified scientific discourse. Private events of the mind are understandable as equivalent to (and emerging in the history of the individual from) observable interaction between biological beings.

The pivotal argument of Mead, which embodied both pragmatism and anti-dualism is that ***mind and self are emergents of the social process.***

> The human being's physiological capacity for developing mind or intelligence is a product of the process of biological evolution . . . but the actual development of his mind or intelligence itself, given that capacity, must proceed in terms of the social situations wherein it gets its expression and import.
>
> (Mead, 1934: 226)

Mead is emphatic that mind and self are products of society. Interpersonal communication comes before the development of the individual's capacity for thought, including the capacity for self-reflection. Here we have the *interactionist* emphasis of 'symbolic interactionists'.

Mead insists that it is the use of language – or, generally, a *symbol* system – which allows the development of mind. Thought and communication are both essentially symbol use. Society provides the symbols.

Essential elements of the social psychology of G.H. Mead

I will describe Mead's theory simply by expounding the three terms of the title of his book *Mind, Self and Society*.

Mind

'Mind' was not a simple synonym of 'brain' for Mead. The brain is a bodily organ; mind is a kind of *activity*. For the individual, the ability to enter into this activity, the process of mind, is possible because of their membership of society. 'Mind-ing' is not a process that the baby is immediately able to carry out. The assumption that the developing infant's brain enables him or her to enter mindfully into social interaction was rejected by Mead:

> If you presuppose the existence of mind at the start, as explaining or making possible the social process of experience, then the origin of minds and the interaction between minds become mysteries. But if, on the other hand, you regard the social process of experience as prior (in a rudimentary form) to the existence of mind and explain the origin of minds in terms of the interaction among individuals within that process, then not only the origin of minds, but also the interaction among minds, cease to seem mysterious or miraculous. Mind arises through communication . . . not communication through mind.
>
> (Mead, 1934: 50)

It is almost built into the name of the discipline, 'psychology', itself to presuppose that its focus is on the individual person. Mead, instead, argued for the priority of the *relationship of communication* between caregiver and infant as the source of the mentality of the infant.

Mead regarded the use of language as developing out of the process of infant–caregiver interaction. It is such symbol use which constitutes the process of mind. Mead's approach certainly overcomes dualism in the sense of a distinction between an inner and an outer world. It also avoids solipsism; the view that individual thinking is from the start a solitary process, and that the sharing of thought between people is what is problematical. Thought arises in a social process, and the individualising of thought is a later development, which is in any case always dependent on the use of the social tool, language. But there are two problems. What sort of communication is possible without 'mind'? And how can the communication thus initiated be 'internalised' so as to allow 'minded activity' to take place?

Mead begins with the un-minded, reflex activity of the newborn child. He argues that here we have a being who is capable of interacting in an elementary way but without the capacity to reflect on the action. The responses of the newborn to the social activity of caregivers can be, as we now know, quite complex (see, for instance, the review edited by Slater and Bremner, 1989). However, Mead suggested that these responses are biologically pre-programmed. They do not depend on thought.

As the infant experiences the responses of others to their early reflex movements, these actions become *gestures*. A gesture in this sense is the initial stage of a piece of behaviour, which gradually stands for the whole action. For instance, the parent leaning over the cot is gradually taken by the infant as 'meaning' the action of lifting. The infant, holding onto the cot rail and bouncing up and down is soon taken as meaning 'lift me up'.

Gesture is a movement which stands for the whole action and it comes to be 'significant'. A *significant gesture* is one that is meaningful to both the interactors. So when behaviour ceases to be a mere reflex and the gesture becomes a sign for a completed act that is meaningful both to the person making the gesture and to the person perceiving it – then we can talk about the meaning of the situation being understood. The development of the pointing gesture is a clear instance of this (Bates *et al.*, 1979). Significance comes about when the imaginary line from finger to the thing being pointed at is understood.

Yet it is spoken and heard language rather than nonverbal behaviour which is the paramount symbol system. Mead points to this as a main basis of *internalisation*. Of course, this term is not supposed to imply that there is a quite separate inner world: rather, it refers to the child's growing capacity to engage in social interaction *covertly*.

It is important to notice that linguistic symbols are a system of shared, not idiosyncratic, meanings. So thinking and external communication are made of the same stuff. Mead expects no problem of translation of thought into word. Note also that, in internalising language the child is not just internalising a symbol system but the system of activity. The process of conversation is being internalised; symbols as part of interaction, or what we will later call *discourse*.

Self

> The self is something which has a development; it is not initially there, at birth, but arises in the process of social experience and activity . . .
>
> (Mead, 1934: 135)

By 'self', Mead refers to two separable things. (a) Self (like mind) is a process – something individuals do. Self is an activity of reflection where the focus of attention is on one's own actions. (b) The self-concept or sense of identity is derivative of self in the first sense. Having acquired the capacity to reflect on one's own actions, one can build up a self-concept or identity.

How does the capacity for self-reflection develop? It is through the reactions of others to the child's behaviour. Firstly, in interaction, one's actions are seen to call forth a response in the other. The other's reactions are, so to speak, an external reflection of one's actions; they are the meaning (for the other) of one's actions. Thereafter it is possible for these meanings to be internalised – an anticipation of the reactions of the other person to one's actions can become established.

I and me. Mead introduces a confusing terminology to cover the internalised self-reflection. It is pictured as a dialogue between an initiating 'I', producing spontaneous and unreflected actions, and an appraising 'me' – which has its origin in the anticipated reactions of the other person. 'I' generates a potential action which is adjusted by the 'me' in the light of the reactions others might have. So the capacity for reflection brought about by mind, the internalisation of symbolic interaction, provides the capacity for reflecting on ourselves.

'Me' can be regarded as a synthesis of others' attitudes. We shall see that Mead allows for the possibility of developing a unified self concept on the basis of others' responses. Then the appraisal of 'I' actions may be in terms of such a self concept rather than directly in terms of the expected reactions of others. The self concept may have a certain autonomy, rather than be changed by each and every response of others to one's behaviour.

Development of the self concept. In symbolic communication there is a growing capacity to take the attitude of the other into account in framing actions. The 'I' is regulated by the 'me', and the resulting actions are appraised for their meaning for other people. The 'me' can be updated by the actual reactions others are seen to have. This means that there is a measure of sophistication in children's awareness of the attitude of others towards themselves. What is happening is that awareness of the self and awareness of others develop hand-in-hand. They are, in fact, part of the very same process. The complexity of the structure of the self concept is increased together with the increasing sophistication of social interaction. Meltzer (1972), see Box 6.1, provides a valuable formulation of Mead's theory of the relationship between the self concept and social interaction.

The self concept as a unity, then, is the range of actions of the individual, viewed in the light of how others-in-general would view them. The unitary *structure* of the self is thought by Mead to develop from social interaction. (And we may expect that

Box 6.1 **G.H. Mead: The co-development of the self and social interaction**

1 *Imitation*. At an early stage of development, the child copies others' actions and expressions. There is no coherent self concept, but here we may see the beginning of 'taking the attitude of the other'.
2 *'Play' stage*. The child taking imaginary roles, and acting 'towards him/herself' from that imaginary external vantage point. This gives the child a basis for perceiving others' responses. Self-awareness is here, but in a rudimentary form. Children have no united perception of themselves as a single self at this stage.
3 *'Game' stage* involves imagining the attitude of a group to oneself. The child begins to cope with situations which call for taking the attitude of a number of people simultaneously. In a team game, for instance, the child has to see him or herself from the vantage point of 'our team' and 'their team' – and, as Goffman (1971) points out, there are an unlimited number of analogies of 'teamplaying' in everyday interaction. The child does not have to experience organised games.

Ultimately, Mead claims, the child is able to take the attitude of the 'generalised other' to him or herself. That is, their activities are appraised by a 'me' that is able to take into account the responses of 'people in general'. With this comes a unified structure of the self.

different societies may lead to variations in the self-structure, cf. Harré, 1976.) The *content* of the self concept involves reflection on oneself.

Society
Mead says relatively little about society as such, and for this reason he comes under the criticism of many sociologists. Mead concentrates on theorising about how the participants in the circle with which the child interacts provide the social experiences which constitute mind and self. Rather than the history and structure of society, Mead's perspective makes interpersonal communication central.

Criticisms

Of course Mead's social psychology was speculative, and awaited evidence. The ***social origin of mind*** now does have support (see Ashworth, 1979). But the details of the process of 'internalisation' are unclear – and, indeed, some interactionists such as Goffman do not regard internalisation as a necessary concept (it smacks of dualism).

Self is exclusively regarded as a social product, yet the reactions of others are not the only form of feedback that infants get as a result of their actions. Self-awareness may not be exclusively social.

Critics differ on whether Mead is too close to ***sociological determinism*** or, seeing social interaction as a nicely poised process of negotiation, too ***voluntaristic*** (see Gonos, 1977; Gillin, 1975).

Erving Goffman

Mead's social psychology combats dualism by locating the origin of the individual mind and selfhood in early social exchange. In contrast, Goffman has almost nothing to say about infancy and childhood. He focuses on the symbolic interaction of adults. Nevertheless, they share a conception of personhood as bound up with membership of society.

What Goffman was trying to do

The primacy of interaction as a research concern. Goffman focused on face-to-face interaction as such, what he called (1983) the 'interaction order' of analysis. Such research would be concerned with interaction rather than the *personalities* of the interactors. Nor would it be concerned (Goffman, 1974) with the *social structure* within which the interaction takes place.

Self is to be regarded as a social presentation. Social behaviour is best analysed in terms of claims to, ascriptions of, and refusals of 'character'. The individual talks and acts in such a way as to claim to be a particular 'kind' of person, and others respond. Interaction essentially involves a *presentation of self*. Note, however, that this absolutely does not mean that there is some underlying self which is being 'expressed' in the presentation. There is no 'inner self' – the presentation is all there is.

Interpersonal validation is necessary. Selves are presented, and are either socially validated or denied. Self is in this way socially regulated (which is not precisely the same as 'socially determined'). The basic human motive for Goffman seems to be the *avoidance of embarrassment*. His social interactor is a conscious agent, concerned with 'face'.

> We must be prepared to see that the impression of reality fostered by a performance is a delicate, fragile thing that can be shattered by very minor mishaps.
>
> (Goffman, 1971: 63)

Some key themes of Goffman's work

Commentators (e.g. Harré and Secord, 1972) tend over-hurriedly to describe Goffman as a 'dramaturgist'. Yet it is only in *Presentation of Self* that he uses the drama as the source of the metaphors employed as a basis for the analysis of social interaction. In other writings, religious ritual (Goffman, 1972b: 47), espionage (1972c), gambling (1972b: 149) and games generally (1972a: 15) are among the resources he employs for carrying out what is essentially the same kind of analysis.

Commentators can also lose a sense of Goffman's underlying consistency (see Ashworth, 1985). But his insistence that the self is a social entity is typically symbolic interactionist. So is the emphasis on the idea that behaviour is to be analysed in terms of its interpersonal meaning.

Action as socially situated and socially meaningful

In every action, a communication is to be accomplished. The person is a *presenter of meaningful action.* To be socially meaningful, action must be bound by certain rules, otherwise it is understandable neither to the actor nor to the audience. Goffman wants to lay out these underlying rules of action.

The self as determined by social arrangements

It is in *Asylums* (Goffman, 1968a) that the author is most profound in his account of the construction of a self in interaction. The book is about interaction within 'total institutions'. That is, prisons, mental institutions, army camps, monasteries and so on; places 'of residence and work where a large number of like-situated individuals, cut off from the wider society for an appreciable length of time, together lead an enclosed, formally administered round of life' (ibid.: 11). In such contexts it may not be surprising that Goffman suggests, first of all, what seems to be a strongly socially determinist picture of the self:

> The self, then, can be seen as something that resides in the arrangements prevailing in a social system for its members. The self in this sense is not a property of the person to whom it is attributed, but dwells rather in the pattern of social controls that is exerted in connection with a person by himself and by those around him. This special kind of institutional arrangement does not so much support the self as constitute it.
>
> (Goffman, 1968a: 154)

Box 6.2 Goffman on homosexuality

In *Stigma: Notes on the Management of Spoiled Identity* (1968b), Goffman discusses the plight of bodily disfigured people and those who are subjected to social persecution, in terms of the dilemmas for self-presentation which their situations pose. There is no discussion of the historical or cultural or broadly political reasons for gender, race or other social discrimination. Nor are any personal motivational dynamics mentioned. Rather, the focus is on interaction.

The bodily disfigurement (e.g. a face spoiled by serious burns) of one of the participants may dominate the situation and subvert the interaction. Similarly, where gender or race is treated as definitive of the person, there is effectively no other way that an individual can present themselves but as an example of that category.

For a homosexual there is a choice of self-presentation. If the choice is not to conceal in self-presentation one's sexual orientation – one decides to 'come out' – then the dynamics of stigma will apply (in a homophobic setting). If, on the other hand, the choice is to remain covert, then stigma is avoided but – in line with the interactionist observation that the individual is their own observer (each person is a kind of mini-community) – this can lead to a discomfort since I am presenting myself in one way (straight) to others and in another way to myself (gay) – 'passing as normal'.

For Goffman either presentation is possible. It is a matter of impression management, not of morality.

The self as constituted by individual role-distancing and choice

In contrast, in a passage in which Goffman discusses ways in which prisoners use legitimate privileges for unintended purposes, he portrays the individual as aware of the self that the institution provides for them, but as *standing apart* from this (role-distancing). So the straightforwardly deterministic account of the way the self is formed by interaction does not exhaust the way self and group are related. 'We always find the individual employing methods to keep some distance, some elbow room, between himself and that with which others assume he should be identified' (Goffman, 1968a: 279).

Goffman finds the social deterministic view of the self far too coarse-grained, for individuals often distinguish between the self implied by the social roles they play, and the attributes they are actually willing to accept and identify with.

In Box 6.2 I bring out some of the implications of Goffman's view of selfhood in the case of homosexuality.

Self-as-performance and consciousness-as-performer

We have a self which is chosen from the range of possibilities which social arrangements provide. The fact that there is choice, however constrained it might be, indicates personal agency 'behind' the selves that are enacted in social encounters, and indeed Goffman says as much:

> Whether the character that is being presented is sober or carefree, of high station or low, the individual who performs the character will be seen for what he largely is, a solitary player involved in a harried concern for his production. Behind many masks and many characters, each performer tends to wear a single look, a naked unsocialised look, a look of concentration, a look of one who is privately engaged in a difficult treacherous task.
>
> (Goffman, 1971: 207)

The task being, of course, self presentation. Commentators on Goffman have objected to this. They either complain that Goffman pays no attention to an 'inner self' (Caudill, 1962), or argue that he seems to be suggesting an aspect of the individual which remains unsocialised (Naegele, 1956). But it is clear that Goffman (1971: 222) divides the individual into two separate entities. The performer is a 'harried fabricator of impressions involved in the all-too-human task of staging a performance'. The self which is performed, in contrast, is 'a figure, typically a fine one, whose spirit, strength and other sterling qualities the performance was designed to evoke'.

The tenuousness of the reality of the encounter: embarrassment and facework

An encounter constructs a reality which is easily destroyed and needs careful attention to sustain. 'There seems to be no agent more effective than another person in bringing a world for oneself alive or, by a glance, a gesture, or a remark, shrivelling up the reality in which it is lodged' (Goffman, 1972a: 38). Others are uniquely placed to threaten the definition of the situation; realities require tender care.

The term 'facework' covers 'the actions taken by a person to make whatever he is doing consistent with face' (Goffman, 1972b: 12). Examples of facework are poise, tact, diplomacy, and *savoir-faire*. Employment of these performances requires the actor to monitor the encounter with circumspection for incipient threats to face. Despite all this guardedness, incidents do occur, and the interaction, together with the selves being performed in it, is thrown into disarray. Embarrassment looms.

Goffman (1972b: 98) writes, 'Whatever else, embarrassment has to do with the figure the individual cuts . . . the crucial concern is the impression one makes on others.' Embarrassment is experienced when the face one is presenting in an encounter is 'discredited'. The interdependence of participants is shown by the fact that it is usually not only the discredited individual who is embarrassed, but the whole group. This is because the discrediting of one person throws the whole encounter out of gear, and mutual self-validation is suspended. Each feels embarrassment on their own account. It is important to act so as to preserve the integrity of the interaction:

> By repeatedly and automatically asking himself the question, 'If I do or do not act in this way, will I or others lose face?' he decides at each moment, consciously or unconsciously, how to behave.
>
> (Goffman, 1972b: 36)

In *Stigma* (1968b), as Box 6.2 indicates, Goffman discusses the plight of bodily disfigured people and those who are subjected to social persecution, in terms of the dilemmas for self-presentation which their situations pose.

Criticisms

Critics have often misunderstood what Goffman was trying to do – so the criticisms need to be considered in the light of the attempt to delineate an area of research focused on *interaction* as such.

Like Mead, there is a ***lack of concern with large-scale society***. Goffman's account of society is lacking on history, social structure, power, and social conflict. It is a 'flat' theory (Giddens, 1988). Can interaction be studied properly like this? Giddens also points out that ***personal motivation*** is not investigated by Goffman. We are certainly socialised – but how, and on the basis of what psychological tendencies?

Goffman's descriptions seem ***cynical***. People, it is presupposed, are Machiavellian deceivers. Partly this comes about through his ironic literary style, partly through the fact that any cool description of behaviour makes it seem more calculative than it is, and partly through the effort to retain the gap between consciousness and selfhood. In essence, what Goffman is saying is that it is irrelevant whether the person engaging in social interaction is saint or con-artist, they must be convincing in getting their presentation accepted.

Goffman implies that the basic categories of interaction must be universal, but the examples are from a restricted range of Anglo-American society. It is possible, therefore, that the work is ***culture-bound***.

Goffman is ***methodologically brazen***, paying no heed to the usual rules of evidence. Nor did he develop a consistent set of concepts, but employed different systems of metaphors which he deemed appropriate to the particular analytic situation.

Discourse analysis and discursive psychology

What discourse analysts are trying to do

Social construction of reality. Reality, for the individual, is constructed by 'discourse': spoken interaction, written material of all kinds, and meaningful actions – and all this can also be referred to broadly as 'text':

> We have tried to show how social texts do not merely *reflect* or *mirror* objects, events and categories pre-existing in the social and natural world. Rather, they actively *construct* a version of those things. They do not just describe things; they *do* things.
>
> (Potter and Wetherell, 1987: 6)

The use of the term 'construction' is intended to highlight the way meaningful action (especially talk) is built from pre-existing socially available discourse. It also points to the individual's participation in the ongoing shaping of the discursive resources of the culture.

It is true that many discourses are so firmly assumed as part of the reality of the everyday social world that almost no one would contest them. Despite this, individuals are users and reconstructors of the discursive resources of the culture, and 'the task of the reconstruction of society can be begun by anyone at any time in any face to face encounter' (Harré, 1979: 405).

Actual human psychology is part of such construction. In their speech and action individuals draw on socially available texts or discourse, and this is no less true when the individual is presenting a self or making a statement about 'psychological' matters. There are socially available resources for presenting oneself as a person. And the employment of these is *what it is to be a person.*

Psychology is a ***hermeneutics*** – an interpretative discipline, not a natural, biological science. The discourse analyst will look for ways in which the speech (and action) of individuals varies and thereby embodies distinct *versions* of the world and of themselves.

Reflexivity is a term, much used by discourse analysts, which means (a) that the dualism which would separate the person who is investigated and the investigator requires demolition. It also points to the fact (b) that the findings of psychology apply to the psychologist as well as to the research participant. It also refers to the idea (c) that the theoretical structures that psychologists build up are themselves discourses.

Knowledge is related to power. Certain assumptions, lines of knowledge, arguments, beliefs are widely taken for granted to be 'common sense'. This can be seen to be related to the positioning of those who purvey such lines.

What is discourse?

The way in which discourse is understood by discourse analysts varies in detail. The aspects of discourse that they stress indicate the specific nature of their research. This is not the place to draw out the distinctions in detail, but the following emphases should be noted.

Following Ricoeur (1971), human meaningful action may be treated as *text*. In this sense, the task of discourse analysis is to 'read' the text. The interest here is on the structure of the discourses as such, rather than on the way in which individuals struggle to make use of them or the details of the social negotiation over their meaning.

One purpose of research, however, is to reveal the currents of belief and argument that are being espoused. Burman and Parker (1993: 4) note the use of the term 'linguistic or interpretative repertoires' in order to emphasise 'the power of conversational context on what people say about themselves from moment to moment'. Such repertoires are, as it were, borrowed from the culture, and shoehorned into the purposes for which they are needed. Potter and Wetherell (1995) emphasise that the way resources are utilised – *discourse practice* – is part of the subject matter of discourse analysis. The construction by people of descriptions of the world can be embedded in actions and activities. Constructions of reality do not have to be explicitly verbalised.

It is expected that there will be variability. Different repertoires will be drawn upon to account for or make sense of different situations as they occur. *Accounting* is achieved through the use of the repertoire(s). Discourse can be described in terms of the *achievement of accounts* since it consists of statements which constitute, for others' acceptance or rejection, an object or event as having such-and-such a set of characteristics. Discourse analysis can focus on *dilemmas* (Billig, 1996), a notion which develops the idea of the achievement of an account, and indicates that people, in presenting a stance, do not simply toe a 'line' but negotiate contrasting material, weighing up, referring to and discounting alternatives. With this emphasis, Billig demonstrates in detail that the venerable discipline of rhetoric becomes relevant, since discursive attempts by an individual are exercises in argument.

Austin (1962) pointed out that in certain formal circumstances it is obvious that to utter a particular form of words is thereby to *do* something. Proposing a toast at a banquet is done simply by the words; similarly to name a child or a ship, or to swear an oath in a court of law. But he went on to say that there is a *performative* impact of all discourse. A function of words and other meaningful actions is not simply to convey information but to have an *effect* (such as the effect in presenting a self that we have already seen explored by Goffman). Viewed in this way, discourse is to be regarded primarily, not as true or false, but as conforming to *felicity conditions* – that is, it aims to be appropriate to the situation in the eyes of participants in the interaction. Of course, a felicity condition in some circumstances might be that the utterance is seen as truthful.

Discursive psychology as hermeneutics

I now want to consider the approach of discourse analysis to the core concepts of psychology. I will call this work *discursive psychology* for present purposes: a sub-area of discourse analysis aimed at a new access to psychology's main concepts. Perceiving, thinking, remembering, motivation and emotion have received the interpretative attention of discursive psychology. A hermeneutics is involved here. For discursive psychology the armoury of mental concepts is regarded as a set of social constructions, of course.

Psychologists, in investigating 'mental processes', set up their theories and experiments on the basis of socially available discourses. For instance, there is a naïve acceptance of what 'remembering' is. In contrast, discursive psychology is concerned precisely with the discourses surrounding mental processes such as remembering. This is not intended by any means as a new route to the discovery of the inner events taking place when such things as remembering occur. Rather, the aim is to describe the way in which claims to be 'remembering' are achieved. Partly, this is to reveal the *felicity conditions* surrounding the claim to be remembering. The question to be tackled would be: What counts as an appropriate instance of 'doing remembering'?

Thinking is, first of all, clarified by removing it from the exclusively inner realm. Entirely in line with Mead, thinking and communication are one and the same (Ashworth, 1979: ch. 3). Thinking draws on the available discourse for its elements – including the use of appropriate (Harré and Gillett, 1994: 43) words and actions to indicate that the utterance is, indeed, 'thought out'. Thoughts are legitimated by their success in producing certain effects within the conversation (even if not actually persuasive, the utterances are treated as instances of 'thought').

Perception is not the starting point in the formation of experience, as it is for cognitive psychology. Rather, the 'extraction of information from the environment' (Harré and Gillett, 1994: 170) is *already* within a social milieu (Ashworth, 1979: ch. 4). 'Information' is already enmeshed in discursive relevances. Discursive psychology, as Potter and Wetherell (1987) have it, moves the centre of psychological attention from *representation* of the world in our awareness through the interpretation of sensory input on the basis of relevant memories, to the discursive repertoires in which we are immersed and in terms of which we live.

Remembering in discursive psychology is different from its treatment in cognitive psychology, as Edwards and Potter argue:

> For discourse analysis, remembering is studied as action, with the report itself taken as an act of remembering, and studiable as a constructed, occasioned version of events. It is studied directly as discourse, rather than taken as a window upon something else that is supposed to be going on inside the reporter's mind.
>
> (Edwards and Potter, 1992: 35)

So again we have the 'mental process' placed firmly in the social world of conversation. The 'rememberer' is uttering a version of events – but rather than being concerned with the mechanism of the 'reach back' into the past, and focusing on the accuracy of the version, discursive psychology takes the act of remembering in its *present* meaning, and in terms of its current function.

To 'be motivated' is not to be subject to certain bodily states which have a determinative effect. Rather, one draws from a socially available 'vocabulary of motives' (Mills, 1940). A person who, in the middle of a furious argument, answers the telephone sweetly, is showing the occasioned and presentational features of a psychological discourse. Ashworth (1979: ch. 7) provides an early example of a discursive psychology of motivation, drawing on Heider's (1958) studies of the commonsense attribution of intention, and going on to show that motive-talk is usually either a matter of repairing a misunderstanding, or a matter of explaining one's choice. In any case it is about managing impressions in interpersonal settings using appropriate reasons, excuses, justifications, and a host of other discursive techniques. More recent attempts in the same vein include Potter and Wetherell (1987: ch. 4), Edwards and Potter (1992), and Harré and Gillett (1994).

To participate in discursive occasions of ***emotion*** is not, it is claimed, to be subject to particular inner processes but to draw on a socially available repertoire of 'emotion behaviour' which will be understood by oneself as well as others as 'indicating' – as it may be – anger. Harré and Gillett (1994: 155) emphasise this feature of emotions: they are 'meaningful displays, performed according to local conventions'. Members of different cultures have different emotions available to them as resources for conveying to themselves and others the 'personal impact' of incidents and events. Most recently, Stearns (1995) has demonstrated the historical and cultural flexibility of the significance of grief.

Discursive psychology and selfhood

Discourse analysts stress that any utterance has among its functions the positioning of the individual within the range of possibilities that the society, the 'discursive community', holds – which leads to a particular approach to the question of homosexuality (see Box 6.3).

Selfhood is a theme which is inextricable from discourse analysis generally. In this vein, feminist researchers have shown how pervasive are the discourses of gender – so that virtually any realm of society has implications for the 'sorts of' female who would be involved in that realm (if women had any legitimate position there at all).

> The question becomes not what is the true nature of the self, but how is the self talked about, how is it theorised in discourse?
>
> (Potter and Wetherell, 1987: 102)

Potter and Wetherall insist that what a person is 'allowed' to be and what they can envisage themselves as being (that is, the possibilities that the relevant discourses hold out for them), are seriously political matters – instances of the exercise of power. In line with this emphasis the individual is regarded as drawing on assumptions about what it is to be a person in achieving their own version of personhood. And among the components that an individual finds available to them are implicit ones – including the grammatical features of the language.

Harré (most recently, 1998) has been prominent in this field, stressing in particular the way in which the grammatical first-

Box 6.3 **Discourses of homosexuality**

For discourse analysts, self-attributions of sexual orientation draw upon socially available discourses. No one can think of themselves as homosexual unless this is a cultural category. And what such an attribution entails – in addition to a sexual preference for members of the same sex (ignominy or acceptance; a distinct personal style of life or unremarkable usualness) – depends on what verbal formulations and trends of action are at hand.

Thus discourse analysts will develop a research programme aimed at eliciting the meanings presented in talk and action which provide – probably several – possible identities for those who (for reasons which themselves are discursive in origin) wish or are driven to take them up.

I say that the origins of such motivation are themselves discursive, for discursive psychology postulates that human motivation is a social matter, grounded in the vocabulary of *kinds of people* which is extant at a particular time in a particular society. It will be clear that there is agreement here with the view of Foucault, discussed in the next chapter, that – if the discourse is lacking – a certain social type does not exist.

person singular encourages the understanding that *I* refers to an entity with agency and personal characteristics. The grammar provides an *I*, and leads one to assume that this points to a substantive entity, the self. However, the truth is that the *I* refers to a kind of social location, not to an inner selfhood.

Finally, Harré and Gillett seem to suggest that not all is text in the analysis of the discursive psychology of selfhood. They draw a distinction between self-constructions and 'the question of our sense of personal individuality' (1994: 102). The latter does not mean the individuality that an individual has simply by being, as it were, at the intersection of a number of discursive positions that may be unique to them. Rather it is graphically illustrated by the nonsensicality of the following situation:

> Could I be mistaken about who I am? Could I wake up one morning and say to myself (whoever that might be!), 'I've discovered that I've been wrong about myself all these years, I am not the person I thought I was. I am after all you.'
>
> (Harré and Gillett, 1994: 103)

The self in this sense is presupposed in the whole of psychology – even discursive psychology. I draw on this meaning of selfhood in the Conclusion.

Criticisms

The model of the text may betray the reality of conversation. The text, according to Ricoeur (1971), refers beyond itself to a world. Not all is text, and not all is construction. If Ricoeur is right, then this undermines the idea of text and discourse employed by discourse analysts. The response of constructionism would be to point out this dilemma: *realism* cannot describe its 'true world' which is said to lie behind constructions without entering into construction itself.

More tellingly, perhaps, the model of the text is an inappropriate one, given the dynamic processes which discourse analysis aims to research; the more appropriate model may be conversation. Harré (1983: 58) is one person associated with this school who takes exactly this line, 'The primary human reality is persons in conversation.'

Socially available discourse is a gloss on the individual lifeworld. Discourse analysis can stop too early. As soon as the various strands of socially available discourse become clear the interviews and the analyses may cease. Deeper research shows that people actively use the discursive resources beyond what is socially given to struggle, on the boundaries of understandability, to make their own sense of the lifeworld.

Discursive psychology subverts psychological science. Since all is supposed to be text, the authors working within other, mainstream psychological viewpoints are treated (dismissively) as merely developing alternative discourses. Of course – rightly or wrongly – this disconnects discursive psychology from the rest of the discipline. Harré is the only author, I think, who attempts integration by speculating on the brain mechanisms, which allow the discursive mind to develop.

Summary: Mead, Goffman, and discourse analysis

- *Consciousness*. Generally, consciousness means linguistically mediated awareness. The social constructionism shared by all the writers discussed in this chapter means that consciousness is not so much a matter of *perception* as it is of deploying socially available repertoires to achieve interaction and to collaborate in the building of intersubjective realities of various kinds.
- *Selfhood*. Mead stresses the process of reflection: the self is that which can be an object of its own awareness. (a) It arises in the process of social interaction. (b) Its structure develops in parallel with the growth in sophistication of interaction, and 'taking the attitude of the other' is a central feature of this.

  For Goffman, selfhood is enacted in the eyes of other people. It is to be understood in terms of the social situations in which it is enacted – social settings hold out a virtual self for their members, and the self is a discursive product. But there is also the tendency to establish individuality of identity.
- *The body*. The meaning of the body is mediated by language and interpretation like any other object in the world. It is a social construction.
- *Other people*. Others are the source of the individual's development of mind and self. It is the other who adjudicates one's claims to selfhood and other 'mental' claims. Authors in this chapter do not regard other people as separated by a gulf of understanding from oneself. Language or discourse is shared, and is the tool, first of communication and then of individual thought.

- *The physical world.* There is no unequivocal reality: the physical world is socially constructed. Accounts of the world are *versions* of reality.

Further reading

Books under G.H. Mead's own name are not the best introduction to his work. There are several edited collections of papers on symbolic interactionism which include articles on Mead. One such is Manis, J.G. and Meltzer, B.N. (1972) *Symbolic Interaction: A Reader in Social Psychology* (Boston: Allyn and Bacon). In contrast to Mead, Goffman's work is readable, fun, and readily available: Goffman, E. (1971) *The Presentation of Self in Everyday Life* (Harmondsworth: Penguin) is basic.

The following overviews of discourse analysis can be recommended:

Potter, J. and Wetherell, M. (1987) *Discourse and Social Psychology: Beyond Attitudes and Behaviour*, London: Sage.
Burman, E. and Parker, I. (eds) (1993) *Discourse Analytic Research: Repertoires and Readings of Texts in Action*, London: Routledge.

Of Rom Harré's many relevant books, these recent volumes are especially interesting: *The Discursive Mind* (with G. Gillett) London: Sage (1994), and *Discursive Psychology in Practice* (with P. Stearns) London: Sage (1995).

Chapter 7

'Human nature' as an outmoded cultural presupposition

chapter 7

Modernity and postmodernity

Modernity is the assumption that ongoing *progress* is possible – or even to be expected. The basis for this lies in the idea that there is a non-negotiable, solid truth or reality about which it is possible to attain ever more accurate knowledge. And it is assumed that human practices can come to conform more and more closely to reality. Modernism characterises both the world of natural science and technology and the social and political world. It is supposed, in modernity, that there are recognised standards of reason by which knowledge advances ever closer to an understanding of reality.

In contrast, postmodernity can be viewed as a cultural movement for which such fixity of criteria of validity of reasoning in all realms is *no longer accepted*, and for which the idea of progress has nothing to refer to, because there is no standard against which to judge an innovation of theory, practice, product or policy which would enable one to see that it is an improvement over what previously existed. Box 7.1 suggests some contemporary cultural features which can be regarded as postmodern.

A relatively early account of postmodernity was published by Jean-François Lyotard (1984). In it, he wrote of the demise of the *grands recits* or overarching narratives of western culture. For instance, the centrality of the individual person as 'hero' of the

***Box 7.1* Some postmodern features of contemporary society**

Self-consciously postmodern art can involve ***lack of adherence to the 'rules'*** of the artform to which it is supposed to belong. Is John Cage's *Four Minutes and Thirty-three Seconds* – in which the performers stay silent – music? One formulation of postmodernism which is relevant here is that a work embodies its own 'rules' and should not be scrutinised for conformity to any external criteria of adequacy.

In line with this, there is no longer universal acceptance of a distinction between ***high art and popular art*** in such areas as music and writing.

Plainly, there can therefore no longer be clarity about the knowledge and understanding appropriate to the education of new members of the culture. One indication of this is that students can study very diffuse modular courses rather than follow a ***syllabus*** upon which all experts agree.

Although ***scientific knowledge*** is the most resistant to postmodernity, there is a tendency for western science to have lost its absolute authority. Thus, alternative therapies seem to be regarded as on a par with orthodox medicine.

In psychology and sociology, the attempt to develop general laws on the model of nineteenth-century physics (***positivism***) is under increasing challenge. Modernism has a strong relationship to positivism, especially in the basic assumption of a solid, unequivocal reality which should be modelled in the theories of all sciences.

There is ***value diversity***. For instance, religious belief is viewed as 'opinion' rather than an account of universal truth.

culture – seen in such narratives as the emancipation of the workers and the steady march of progress leading to the classless society, and also in the image of the entrepreneur and the accumulation of wealth – is under challenge. Another *grand recit* is the notion of a disinterested search for truth, shown in such narratives as the progress of scientific research with its promise of the mastery of nature, and Marx's scientific socialism. All these narratives are bound up with the idea of an underlying true reality and therefore the possibility of progress, and postmodernism rejects them.

For Lyotard, postmodernism entails a fragmentation within the society, a lack of consensus. More positively, in Lyotard's final pages, it means a certain emancipation of human activity. Not legitimised by definite sets of rules – standards by which it would be possible to judge straightforwardly whether (to revert to our own concerns) a piece of work was 'good psychology' – a work has to embody in its own production some hint as to what it is about.

Psychology and postmodernism (1)

A further event within contemporary culture reinforces the postmodern attitude. This is the growth within semantics – the theory of linguistic meaning – of the view that the meaning of words and sentences is not based on their representation of facts in the real world. Rather, according to Derrida for instance, there is nothing outside the 'text'. The truth of a piece of discourse cannot be independently validated, but can at best only be translated into another segment of discourse. We have already seen, in our discussion of discourse analysis in the previous chapter, the way that this viewpoint has affected some work in psychology very fundamentally. This is not to say that all discourse analysis or discursive psychology is postmodernist.

Plainly, most psychology – certainly the forms of it discussed in the first four chapters of this book – is modernist in its assumptions. There is a true reality to be uncovered by the activities of researchers, and findings at one moment in time are the stepping stones to refined findings later on. Postmodern thinking questions this (see Kvale, 1992), and an important implication is that psychology can no longer present itself as 'outside human society, looking in'. It is not detached, but part of the Babel of discourses within the culture. And, as we saw in Chapter 6, discursive psychology does not pretend to progressively reveal true, universal human nature, but attempts to make us aware of the implicit assumptions about persons that are available to the members of a social group for the time being.

Hermeneutics: a method for postmodernism

If the postmodern attitude is adopted, how can we proceed? Hermeneutics seems to provide a way, since the focus of research work must be the uncovering and interpretation of meanings. One source of contemporary hermeneutics is found in the work of Heidegger, and I must now indicate the direction which a relevant part of his work takes.

The first thing to grasp about this thinker is his rejection of the *correspondence theory* of truth. This is the view that we can regard something as true when (a) the *representation* of something in thought and theory corresponds with or matches (b) *reality*. It can immediately be seen that this assumes that a criterion of reality can be found which lies outside the 'representation'. It can be seen that the psychological notion of validity is a version of the correspondence theory of truth. But if there is only 'representation' – discourse, or text – and there is no underlying reality free of interpretation, the correspondence theory of truth will not work. (It is for this reason that the psychological notion of validation cannot be applied to the findings of discourse analysis; there is no independent criterion against which to judge the correctness of the findings.)

The interpretations which result from hermeneutic work, then, have to be judged in terms of their coherence (they hang together and make sense as a whole) and in terms of the new light that they seem to shed on something that is otherwise obscure. So Freud's dream theory – which I argued in Chapter 2 was at least in part a set of hermeneutic rules for interpretation – is to be judged by its value in illuminating the manifest content.

Now Heidegger argued that the process of interpretation is an everyday feature of human activity. Human beings are from the start immersed in the world (Heidegger [1962] uses the term *Being-in-the-world* to refer to entities of the human kind), and from the start we are engaged in *interpreting* it. The human being is inescapably 'hermeneutic'; we are interpreters.

In interpretation there are always *presuppositions*, which determine the direction of interpretation:

> In interpreting, we do not, so to speak, throw a 'signification' over some naked thing which is present-at-hand, we do not stick a value on it; but when something within-the-world is encountered as such, the thing in question already has an involvement which is disclosed in our understanding of the world, and this involvement is one which gets laid out by the interpretation.
>
> (Heidegger, 1962: 190–191)

Interpretation depends on standpoint, and the meaning of something has to be in terms of the relevance of the thing to the interpreter. So a cycle of interpretation is observed everywhere. This *hermeneutic circle* begins with our engagement with something in our world on the basis of a fore-understanding (or, we might say, the discourses with which we are familiar). Further interpretation, on the basis of greater involvement or experience with that thing, then illuminates, revises, enriches the initial understanding. Our new understanding can then be the starting point for future interpretative efforts.

In *Truth and Method*, Gadamer (1975) developed Heidegger's thinking on hermeneutics. The discussion below is specifically about history, but the issue is precisely the same when it comes to psychology, since the question is of the possibility of the human understanding of another person. In Weinsheimer's summary of Gadamer:

> The question arises as to whether acquiring a historical horizon [i.e. the acquisition of a general grasp of a particular

> past period] means placing ourselves within the horizon of a past tradition so that we could understand it with its own eyes, from its own perspective. Clearly, acquiring a historical horizon does not mean that at all. We exist nowhere but in our own time, within our own horizon, and there is no magical time machine that can transport us anywhere else.
>
> (Weinsheimer, 1985: 182–183)

The emphasis of Gadamer is clear. There can be no general rules of hermeneutics (since each interpretation is inevitably bound by a specific 'fore-understanding'). And our access to other cultures – or, indeed, our psychological access to other people – cannot be through attempting to take the attitude of the other culture or person. Rather we must recognise that we take our presuppositions to the study, and should see our understanding of the others as a kind of convergence, whereby our assumptions guide our approach to research, but that the phenomenon being studied challenges the assumptions so that we end up with a revision of understanding. In effect, research work does not provide us with facts about the person or thing being researched; rather, it leads to an adustment of our prejudices. And it is not just that 'objectivity' is a hard quality to achieve, but that it is impossible – not least because there is *no unequivocal reality* to be sought. Gadamer's elaboration of Heidegger gives pride of place to culture in the form of the available discourses on the basis of which we understand. For the researcher, it is from the standpoint of discourse that all interpretation begins and ends.

Psychology and postmodernism (2)

In earlier pages devoted to Freud, Skinner and discursive psychology, I showed how various authors use their own theoretical framework to interpret 'psychological processes'. We can see now that hermeneutic theory would not expect convergence among these research programmes towards the 'true reality' of thinking, perceiving, dreaming, etc. Instead, they are to be seen as independent interpretative activities, each with their own fore-understandings about human nature, and each developing deepened but different 'bodies of knowledge'. There would be convergence if there were an uncontrovertible, solid reality to which all the interpretative attempts were directed, however different their starting points. But postmodernism excludes this.

What we have, in the sections of previous chapters labelled 'hermeneutics', is the author's interpretation, taking off from a specific fore-understanding of human nature and building an increasingly sophisticated but never final version of psychology within that horizon.

We now turn our attention to two specific postmodern writers whose work brings out some of the implications of this viewpoint for the understanding of (what will be a problematical term for them) 'human nature' – Foucault and Derrida.

Michel Foucault and the archaeology of knowledge

What Foucault was trying to do

His intention can best be understood by coming to a realisation of the meaning of the following apparently opaque statement:

> My aim was to analyse this history [of thought], in the discontinuity that no teleology would reduce in advance; . . . to allow it to be deployed in an anonymity on which no transcendental constitution would impose the form of the subject; to open it up to a temporality that would not promise the return of any dawn. My aim was to cleanse it of all transcendental narcissism . . .
>
> (Foucault, 1972: 202–203)

The first feature of the above quote which deserves our attention is that Foucault sees the ***history of thought as discontinuous and with no direction or purpose***. Although Foucault's work varies in the extent to which history is treated as discontinuous, the idea of teleology (development towards a future goal, where the goal dictates the direction of development) is consistently avoided.

The thought of a period of history is impersonal. It should be analysed without regard to particular individuals, for it is the culture as a whole which must be seen to have a particular 'outlook'. What is more, the study of the history of thought must be ***detached from concern for the mental life*** of members of the culture. Foucault especially rejects (in line with Gadamer) the idea that the truth of historical understanding can be guaranteed by present-day readers sympathetically 'entering into' the experience of the participants. In this context, it is regarded by postmodernists generally as essential to reject the Husserlian phenomenological approach to knowledge that we saw in Sartre (Chapter 5). They absolutely deny that one can discover facts about reality by carefully analysing human experience. Experience is *within* discourse; it cannot be a criterion of the accuracy of discourse. To think otherwise is 'transcendental narcissism' – human self-aggrandisement through the exaltation of supposed structures of the mind.

Additionally, Foucault is throughout concerned to show ***the roots of contemporary, modern discourse and reveal its fundamentally coercive nature.*** We shall see that he concerns himself with the social 'rational' control of the individual. To be able to claim *knowledge* is to have power. Psychology and its associated technologies – social work, criminology, psychiatry, etc. – are part of the modern attempt at a *bureaucratisation* of the individual, moulding and controlling the person.

Foucault's work and the interpretation of 'human nature'

I will try to show how Foucault uncovers the way in which human nature was understood in previous epochs by selectively describing particular lines of work.

Madness and Civilization (1971), and the history of 'insanity'

Foucault inaugurated a new area of historical research by looking at the cultural assumptions underlying the way 'mental illness' has

Box 7.2 Foucault and discontinuities in the western understanding of 'madness'

Medieval view of madness as sacred: The person deemed mad was seen as a 'holy fool'; during the Renaissance this view was maintained. Madness was a special kind of ironical, elevated reason: the wisdom of folly (cf. Don Quixote).

Mid-seventeenth-century move towards hospitalisation: The mental hospital was not intended to be therapeutic but to confine the mad until they had been 'corrected'. The insane were isolated from the sane, though not driven out entirely – simply held in separate institutions.

In the *late eighteenth century reforms* started. The insane were now viewed differently from other deviants (whereas previously madness and criminality were both versions of abnormality) and attempts at therapy began. Foucault evaluates this reform, surprisingly, negatively. From his perspective, not only were bodies now confined and excluded, but therapy meant that there was even an attempt to capture the minds of the mad.

The *contemporary world blurs the distinction between sanity and madness* – it is a continuum, with a variety of neuroses (each having different degrees of impact on society and the person). The idea of a continuum weakens the attitude that calls for the mad to be confined to an 'asylum'. But it means that the scope for 'doctors of the mind' of a number of kinds becomes greater – no one is quite sane. Therapy becomes ever more pervasive.

been dealt with. He claims that 'the' discourse on insanity has gone through a number of discontinuous phases (see Box 7.2).

Foucault (1971) is concerned with a *'presentist'* history, trying to uncover the roots of contemporary discourse. So the perspective is necessarily different from that of a historian whose work is focused on understanding a particular past epoch. Nevertheless, critics dispute the 'historical facts'. The phases are not as clear-cut as Foucault pretends (for instance, some kind of therapy was often attempted during the seventeenth century). There is more continuity across periods than Foucault presumed, and more variety within periods too. And Foucault's interpretation of the changes as moving from permissiveness to an increasingly intrusive and bureaucratic rationalism is inadequate to account for the facts. Finally, the evaluation of eighteenth-century reforms as repressive is perverse.

Now we are in a quandary. Can a postmodern account be criticised for its lack of historical accuracy? Such attacks assume a solid past reality about which one can be correct or wrong. And in any case, as I have said, Foucault – here in the spirit of Gadamer – is providing a story of the past intended to illuminate the present rather than be 'accurate'. On our decision as to the resolution of dilemmas like this our appraisal of postmodernism generally must be based.

Birth of the Clinic (Foucault, 1973a) is a book from the same period of Foucault's work, and is concerned with the different historical perceptions of the body and of disease. It is of interest here in moving towards a new way of thinking about history – one which was not so evident in *Madness and Civilisation*. It considers the wider social context of medical thought and practice, and tries to show how medical discourse is 'articulated' (links and connects) with other institutions and activities.

The '*Archaeology*' and epistemes

The Order of Things (1973b) does not continue with the 'articulation' theme, but analyses discourses in order to disinter (hence 'archaeology') the underlying conceptual system – the basic, impersonal, unconscious cultural codes which provide an order for experience. These codes are 'epistemes'. Foucault chooses to examine natural history/biology, economics, and grammar/philology – and searches for what he assumes there must be: strong similarities (at some level) between these three areas within a given period, constituting the period's episteme.

Epistemes are radically different from each other, and changes from one to the next are fundamental shifts in thinking.

Box 7.3 Four world-views and the rise (and fall) of psychological science

Pre-classical, to mid-seventeenth century, with its ***Renaissance episteme.*** Here words and things are part of a unified whole, and words and things relate to each other in terms of resemblances or correspondences. For example, analogies between words and things signified real connections: so 'signatures', maybe found in the shape of the leaf, indicated the appropriateness of certain plants for treating certain diseases.

The mid-seventeenth century suddenly saw the end of the episteme of resemblances. 'The activity of mind . . . will therefore no longer consist in *drawing things together*, in setting out on a quest for everything that might reveal some sort of kinship, attraction, or secretly shared nature within them, but, on the contrary, in *discriminating*, that is, establishing their identities' (Foucault, 1973b: 55). The 'classical' episteme was concerned with ***ordering and classifying***; this is the period of Linnaeus's biological taxonomy. Foucault stresses that the episteme of this period did not treat *Homo sapiens* as ontologically distinct.

The late eighteenth century until the end of the Second World War, the 'modern' age, saw the movement from a 'tabular' to a ***'dynamic' episteme.*** Rather than ordering, historicising takes precedence – the time dimension comes to the fore, stressing evolution, production and the roots of language. It is in this context that the human being becomes identified as a specific object of discourse. This development – which included the rise of psychology – is to be regarded as simply a feature of the modern episteme.

The contemporary world, since 1950, is postmodern, in which, Foucault suggests (though the book hardly deals with the contemporary episteme), we see the eclipse of individual experience as the basis of truth. (We might provide the example here, that scientific theories do not need to be 'understandable'; they can arise from the working-through of mathematical models with no direct relation to experience.)

The thinking of one episteme is not understandable to another. Discontinuities are stressed. There is *no idea of progress* from one historical episteme to another; simply change. Similarly, Foucault has *no concept of objectivity*. Four epistemes are delineated during the period Foucault covers, and these are outlined in Box 7.3. Of particular interest is the claim that human beings were delineated as distinct relatively late on, and that this attention to the individual is in decline (a point emphasised at the end of the book and which I will discuss later).

Again, Foucault is concerned with the past – not for its own sake, but to elucidate contemporary knowledge. But his historical facts are inaccurate, it seems, so the same line of criticism can be made as for *Madness and Civilisation*. Additionally the lack of discussion of the physical sciences and mathematics misses ways of thinking that contradict particularly tellingly Foucault's account.

Following his slightly later *Archaeology of Knowledge* (1972), Foucault implicitly acknowledged the criticisms of his analysis of the conceptual forms underlying historical epochs as too monolithic. He drops the notion of epistemes, and replaces it with an assertion of the primacy of *discourse*. So it is possible to refer to discourse-space, meaning a particular realm of social cognition and practical activity with its own rationality.

Importantly, for Foucault the power of discourse comes not from the individual speaker-actor. Discourse constrains and even constitutes the individual. Note that discourse does not differentiate science and ideology. (If it did, the notion would cease to be postmodern.) At this stage, Foucault starts focusing on the relationship between knowledge and power, or discourse and control. There is *external* control of the individual in that 'everyone' recognises that there are only certain doable and sayable things. There is also *inner* control, since the very sense of self is located within the historical discourse-space of what a person is taken to be.

Discipline and Punish (1977), and Foucault's account of power

The history of punishment in this book begins with the pre-nineteenth century, which Foucault characterises as typified by public torture, in which control is exercised through physical terror. Subsequently, rational reform associated with the Enlightenment involved a new understanding of crime. It was not now seen as a personal attack on the sovereign but as a breach of the social contract which underpinned civil society. New methods of punishment were aimed at restoring the wrong done to society, and restoring the criminal to their lawful place in it. In this context, punishment must be seen as non-arbitrary, justifiable. But Foucault is again adamant that reforming humanitarianism is basically concerned with control and power. There is, in effect, greater coercive value in a system which all are logically bound to agree is legitimate than in the despotic exercise of terror.

Reformed incarceration entailed as thoroughgoing an *observation* of the prisoner as possible. Bentham's 'panopticon' – a prison architecture in which all inmates were simultaneously visible to the warders – is an example of the aim of observation to maintain control and establish discipline. The prison is a clear case, but Foucault lists other foci for the institutionalised imposition of power. Factory, hospital and school he sees as being similar, in making concrete the discourse of discipline.

Similar issues of historical accuracy arise in this work as in the studies of clinical medicine and the treatment of insanity, and there are similar complaints concerning the one-sided interpretation of reform as fundamentally coercive and intrusive of the individual.

Note that control is, for Foucault, by no means exclusively exercised through discourses of punishment. Much control, in the form of guidance, is 'for their own good'. Even more control is exercised through arrangements that are willingly entered into by individuals because they make for comfort, health, security, etc. And, most importantly in his concluding writings, the production of *individuals themselves* is within a discourse-space with associated controls. A culture has intrinsic understandings of what it is to be a person, and in terms of which individuals are constructed.

The History of Sexuality (1981, 1987, 1990) and the discursive self

Foucault's last, uncompleted, work is in some ways far less strident, and far more scholarly. But it also makes the point about control-through-discourse (i.e. knowledge/power) even more

Box 7.4 Foucaultian theory and discourses of homosexuality

For Foucault, the realm of *what is* is the realm of discourse. Thus, in cultures in which the element 'homosexual', as designating the sexual orientation of a person, does not exist, then no one is 'a homosexual'. This is not to say that *activities and affections* that could be so designated do not occur (they may even be separately characterised in discourse) but a *person* is not characterised as such.

When such discourse did emerge, then those who found themselves open to its labelling employed exactly the same categories as the repressive society – though with reversed intention. Thus we have an instance of the construction of identity, and the formulation of a demand that such an identity should be accepted, from socially available discourse:

> The appearance in nineteenth-century psychiatry, jurisprudence, and literature of a whole series of discourses on the species and subspecies of homosexuality . . . made possible a strong advance of social controls into this area of 'perversity'; but it also made possible the formation of a 'reverse' discourse: homosexuality began to speak in its own behalf, to demand that its legitimacy or 'naturality' be acknowledged, often in the same vocabulary, using the same categories by which it was medically disqualified [i.e. ruled unacceptable]. There is not, on the one side, a discourse of power, and opposite it, another discourse that runs counter to it. Discourses are tactical elements . . .
>
> (Foucault, 1981: 101)

strongly because it argues cogently that the discourse-space of sexuality is one in which the individual defines *himself or herself*. Foucault finds it no accident that morality gets treated most centrally as sexual morality, for in the self-examination that awareness of sexuality entails, a process of personal self-monitoring is established: a kind of inner panopticon. Foucault's account of the Christian era shows an increasing emphasis on confession, and later (with Protestantism) self-examination. Earlier norms of confession limited it to the occasional examination of external indications of propriety, and it was infrequent. Later, it became linked with self-scrutiny.

Foucault regards the idea of personal sexuality as developing in tandem with the emergence of the modern individual self, and self-scrutiny within a discourse of sexuality becomes a powerful mechanism of control. Note that this is not anything to do with Freudian notions of the repression of sexuality and the development of the individual superego. Sexuality is, for Foucault, *produced* within a particular discursive milieu, and the attempt to locate the self within this discourse is itself productive of unhappiness. Plainly, our ongoing use of homosexuality as an example of the application of the theories is particularly apposite here (see Box 7.4).

Derrida and deconstruction

What Derrida was trying to do

Derrida's postmodernism, like Foucault's, is aimed at the ***eradication of the idea that truth is grounded in the clarification of individual experience***. He further argues that there is a pervasive form of prejudice in favour of individual experience which entails prioritising speech over cultural forms which are not directly linked to 'the speaker'. He calls this prejudice *logocentrism*. Writing is at a remove from the 'thinking' of the person – and therefore tends to be implicitly devalued. There is, for Derrida, residual humanism in this prejudice. He tries to show that ***writing is as basic as speaking***.

Yet this is not to say that we can find some unequivocal source of truth in writing. Rather, with ***deconstruction***, Derrida can be seen as doing very radical hermeneutics – but a hermeneutics which comes out *in principle* with the claim that we cannot finally know what is meant. The effort to show in a particular case the undecidability of a piece of writing is 'deconstruction'.

Whereas Foucault was, at least at one stage, interested in the articulation between discourse and other social features, Derrida regards all as, in the end, discourse. This also contrasts with Freud who, in Ricoeur's account, aimed at grounding interpretation in the biological processes of libido. For Derrida there is ***no hermeneutically privileged realm*** – some area of knowledge in which the certainty of absolute truth can be found. All is text and all is equivocal.

Writing and speech

Text and personal expression

The distinction between writing and speech is not easily drawn (of course! – it is itself ultimately undecidable). But the main issue seems to be about speech as being the personal expression of experience, and therefore relating closely to the 'presence' of external reality to the speaker. Writing is removed from direct experience. The better forms of writing are closest to speech (the 'written word'), so Plato wrote dialogues.

Maybe the strongest account of his rejection of the prejudice in favour of speech is Derrida's (1981) deconstruction of part of the *Phaedrus* by Plato. In that work, Plato tries at length to show how much speech is to be preferred over writing. Plato recounts a myth in which the Egyptian King Thamus is offered the gift of writing by the god Thoth. Thamus rejects it, with the following arguments. Spoken language is a living, real presence, whereas writing is dead inscription. Powers of memory would decline; authentic wisdom would be replaced by mere knowledge; students would be able to be widely read without the benefit of a teacher's instruction. And, in spoken discussion, people can be questioned about what they mean; a book is not interactive.

In his deconstruction of Plato's *Phaedrus*, Derrida tries to show how anomalous this rejection of writing is. It cannot be unequivocally understood. Why does Plato use myth (a form of which he is otherwise disdainful as being an inadequate vehicle for the truth – effectively a form of writing)? Why does Plato use phrases in praise of spoken language such as 'written in the heart' (using a metaphor drawn from the very thing which is being criticised)? Most tellingly, Plato is guiltily condemning writing *in writing*.

Derrida particularly likes to meditate on the use by philosophers of words with reversible senses, and discusses at length a term which Plato uses in connection with writing, *pharmicon*, which has two chief meanings: 'poison' and 'cure' (cf. 'drug'). Translators pick the alternative that seems to them to fit best in a given context, but Derrida insists on maintaining the ambiguity of writing as both poison and remedy.

Texts, intertextuality and the universality of textuality

The writing *per se* is to be addressed in Derrida's work. There is no recourse to the modernist insistence that texts have authors and that the hermeneutic aim should be to uncover the intention of the author. That rests on the prejudice in favour of experience and the prioritising of speech. Further, texts should not be regarded as delimited by the 'authority' of their official presentation. In *Of Grammatology* (1976), Derrida points out that a *book*, for instance, is supposed to be taken as the self-sufficient utterance of its author. But as discourse the text relies on its relationship to other texts; indeed, the meaning of the text is for the most part interpretable only by its implied reference to other texts. And the interpretations which are possible of it are themselves, of course, textual. There is no escape, as it were, onto solid ground. What would 'solid ground' be?

Derrida and the deconstruction of psychology

Of course, Derrida could turn his attention to the writings of psychological authors and demonstrate the ultimate undecidability of their statements. Many of them, for instance, could be shown to make use of the pronoun *I* in a way that asks the reader to assume that the writer is a rational conscious agent, while the theory they are expounding pictures individuals as anything but this. Derrida could also criticise, in the manner of the discourse analysts, the claim of many psychologists to be uncovering a true underlying reality: human nature. This idea is thoroughly problematical for all postmodern thinkers.

Criticisms

Irrationality, normlessness, political standpointlessness

Postmodernity is playfully irresponsible in its denial of values and criteria of judgement. All such criteria are held to be examples of an underlying power rationale of all discourse. Postmodernism is profoundly relativist and gives us no basis for the choice of one narrative or discourse over another. For this reason, Habermas (1987) has claimed that it is 'neo-conservative': demystifying and critically analysing culture is only of emancipatory value if there is some standard by which valid knowledge can be judged, but postmodernists offer no justification of an alternative to the social status quo. All that can be done is to snipe, and to relativise.

Anti-humanism or a way of emancipation?

As I mentioned in discussion of Foucault on the history of knowledge, he took the view that the idea of 'the person' is of 'recent invention':

> One thing in any case is certain: man is neither the oldest nor the most constant problem that has been posed for human knowledge. Taking a relatively short chronological

> sample within a restricted geographical area – European culture since the sixteenth century – one can be certain that man is a recent invention within it. . . . As the archaeology of our thought easily shows, man is an invention of recent date. And one perhaps nearing its end.
>
> (Foucault, 1973b: 386–387)

What are the implications of the deconstruction of the 'subject' – the human agent? For both Derrida and Foucault, the individual self is to be regarded as the product of the discourses in which it is situated. If there is no socially available discourse of human nature then there *is* no human nature. And the modes of humanity available to us – if we are members of a culture in which self-definition is required – are just those of our society.

There are two conflated purposes in this postmodernist attack on the self. One of them is not dissimilar from that of Sartre; for him also, the self is extrinsic to consciousness, though he does not tie our construction of a self to discourse. The other purpose is more radical. Here the attack is on the view of personal awareness as giving access to truth. The postmodernists regard this attitude as giving rise to the notions of both objectivity (as awareness shorn of bias) and subjectivity (the personal perspective) – both of which they regard as pernicious.

Given the rejection of the human standpoint, both as source of truth and as a basic value, it is somehow contradictory that postmodernist writers see themselves as concerned with emancipation. What for?

Summary

I ought, in line with the rest of the book, appraise postmodernist social theory in terms of the views it adopts on what we have treated as the main categories of human reality. But these categories themselves are, of course, open to deconstruction. What *discourse* constitutes these categories as being 'the main categories of human reality'?

Consciousness, the body, selfhood, other people, the physical world . . .

The *'grand recit'* (Lyotard) underlying a book about 'human nature' would seem to be the centrality of the person. This is revealed, for instance, in the list which I have used to summarise each of the chapters. It has a built-in theme implying certain presuppositions about what human nature is. It starts with individual consciousness and 'works outward'.

If this offers a line of critique of the book itself in its interpretation of 'human nature', there is a more radical criticism available in postmodernism, which touches psychology generally. The very idea of 'human nature', according to the postmodernists, is to be treated as a feature of the discourse of a particular culture at a particular time. Maybe there will soon be no such thing as 'human nature', as Foucault proclaims. And for postmodernists this does not simply mean that there will be no more talk about it, no more writing about it, and no more power in the concept. Rather, since there is nothing outside the text, there will be *no such thing* as 'human nature'.

Further reading

Most of Foucault's writing is of direct relevance to the question of human nature, but see Merquior, J.G. (1985) *Foucault* (London: Fontana) for an overview. In so far as his work is relevant to our question, Derrida is made as clear as he can be by Norris, C. (1987) *Derrida* (London: Fontana). Both of these books are in the *Modern Masters* series.

The most accessible account of postmodernism for psychologists is the book edited by Kvale, S. (1992) *Psychology and Postmodernism* (London: Sage).

Chapter 8

Conclusion

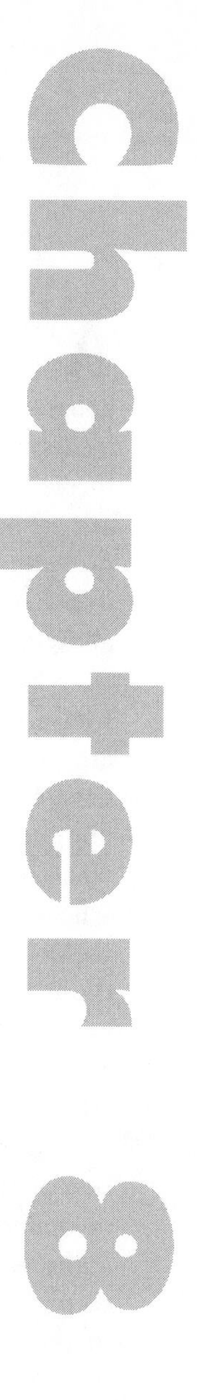

ALL THE THEORIES DISCUSSED in the pages of this book are alive in the sense that they each contribute to contemporary debate on human nature, but some indication of their historical location might be valuable. Box 8.1 provides something along these lines. However, in this Conclusion, I do not wish to carry out a final critical review of these theories. I will, instead, shortly present a personal perspective on what I take to be some central issues of human nature – issues which I believe we should not allow ourselves to forget.

Before this, however, a word more about the blind eye which I have turned to history in the course of this book. The chapters are not arranged historically; I have rarely referred to historical debates or historical sequence within the chapters, and – while not going as far as one eminent teacher is reported to have done when lecturing on Aristotle (he 'was born, worked, and died') – I have not traced the flux of authors' views and located them within their biography. Increasingly, disapproval is expressed of those who comment on theories without locating them historically or biographically. It is said that only in such contexts can scholarly thought and even 'objective' scientific thought be properly appraised.

In my view this opinion is exaggerated. In any case, the location of an author's thought within the ebb and flow of the currents of opinion and other influences of the time, and also within that author's personal concerns, can hardly fix the interpretation of their theory. How could it? But there is a more immediate basis of the understanding of a theory for us. That is the one which we – as readers and interpreters – bring, locating it within *our own* personal concerns and relevances.

Therefore I wish to explicitly invite the reader to enter into debate with the standpoint of the book in general and with the views of each of the authors presented in it. For it seems to me

Box 8.1 **Some major authors and publication dates**

1. The Ultimate Biological Motive: The Evolutionary Perspective
   - C. Darwin (1809–1882) *The Origin of Species by Means of Natural Selection* (1859)
   - E.O. Wilson (1929–) *Sociobiology: The New Synthesis* (1975)

2. Mental Conflict: Biological Drives and Social Reality
   - S. Freud (1856–1939) *Die Traumdeutung* (dated 1900, actual publication 1899; trans. *The Interpretation of Dreams*, 1913)

3. An Inner World: Cognitive Psychology
   - The study of cognitive processes does not have a clear founding figure. Two influential texts are:
   - F.C. Bartlett, *Remembering: A Study in Experimental and Social Psychology* (1932)
   - U. Neisser, *Cognitive Psychology* (1967)

   On cognitive 'content' see:
   - G.A. Kelly (1905–1967) *The Psychology of Personal Constructs* (1955)

4 . . . Not Separable from the World: Skinner's Radical Behaviourism
   - B.F. Skinner (1904–1990) *Science and Human Behaviour* (1953)

5 The Individual Consciousness: Anxiously Free in a Meaningless World
   - J.-P. Sartre (1905–1980) *L'Etre et le Néant* (1943); trans. *Being and Nothingness* (1958)

6 Social Being: Interacting, and Presenting Oneself as a Person
- G.H. Mead (1863–1931) *Mind, Self and Society*, (posthumous, 1934)
- E. Goffman (1922–1982) *The Presentation of Self in Everyday Life* (1956)

7 'Human Nature' as an Outmoded Cultural Presupposition
- M. Heidegger (1889–1976) *Sein und Zeit* (1927); trans. *Being and Time* (1962)
- G.-H. Gadamer (1900–) *Wahrheit und Methode* (1960); trans. *Truth and Method* (1975)
- M. Foucault (1926–1984) *L'Archéologie du Savoir* (1969); trans. *The Archaeology of Knowledge* (1972)
- J. Derrida (1930–) *L'Ecriture et la Différence* (1967); trans. *Writing and Difference* (1978)

a matter of some seriousness to either adopt or reject a view of human nature – especially if this is done *deeply*, affecting one's own view of oneself and others. Additionally it is a founding value of western higher education that human conceptualisations – all of them, with no limits of sacredness or taboo – are always and everywhere *contestable*. This is a view I fervently hold. In Box 8.2 I therefore suggest some lines of thought which may encourage such debate and critique.

The orientation of this book has indeed been to stir puzzlement, curiosity, and critique. In trying to do this I have avoided the approach of mainstream empirical psychology – proceeding from experimental study to experimental study in a search, through piecemeal accumulation of evidence, for the whole picture. This modernist way of tackling the question of human nature is governed by the assumptions of its starting point, and would not enable that wide variety of viewpoints, which I feel genuinely contribute to the question of the meaning of human

Box 8.2 **Debating with the book: some issues for consideration**

All books are written from a point of view, of course. The reader might consider the following issues in order to *interact* with this point of view; to debate with it:

1. The mainstream psychologist will judge claims about some aspect of human behaviour in terms of the strength of *experimental evidence*. What are the presuppositions about human nature which the prioritising of such evidence carries with it? Are these presuppositions justifiable?
2. Could the more speculative assertions of some of the authors in this book be framed as research hypotheses? Among those that cannot, do you regard any as worth consideration? Are there ways in which they could be argued for persuasively?
3. This book has been roughly arranged in terms of two parameters: biology versus society, and determinism versus voluntarism. What other parameters might be useful? What selection of writers would be included and excluded? Would different disciplines be included?
4. I have summarised each view of human nature in terms of the stance taken on consciousness, selfhood, other people, the body, and the physical world. Suggest a different set of phenomena on which to compare theories. Would you remove some of mine? Why?
5. What do your responses to the matters raised above say about your own approach to the question of human nature?
6. Maybe one of the views discussed in this book comes closest to your own viewpoint. How would you adjust it to concord with yours more exactly? What would your alterations do to the argument of the original theory?
7. Does a personal view of human nature matter?

nature, to be discussed. There is a sense, therefore, in which this very plan of approach to the question of human nature is postmodern (for instance, the idea that there is a fixed set of criteria of adequacy of theories has been suspended). Yet I have some hesitations regarding a strong postmodern position.

Language, intersubjectivity and individual creativity

Firstly, though I would not dissent from the postmodern emphasis on the centrality of language – and the culture it embodies – to human nature, I cannot accept the position of Derrida regarding the exclusive and pervasively paramount nature of the text. Text *has* an outside. In particular, it assumes certain realities which are essential to our experience of any world whatsoever. These include ones that are central to the study of human nature: consciousness, identity, embodiment, the assumption of people's real existence (intersubjectivity), and the presupposition of the 'outer' world.

There is no doubt diversity in the way in which these truths of experience are found in discourse, but they *have to be there*. Of course, it is because of their solid reality in the lifeworld that I chose them as the basis for summarising the theories covered in this book.

These are, therefore, instances of essential features of any understanding of human nature whatsoever. Complete relativity is wrong since language must echo these (and doubtless other) essential categories. Of course, in so doing, a particular language will propagate a particular version of them. Users of a particular language are given the opportunity to see their world from a certain perspective.

The constraint on languages – that they relate to a world with certain essential parameters – does not in itself contradict the linguistic determinism that is emphasised by the interactionists and discourse analysts of Chapter 6. But is it wholly the case that the categories of my language cannot be transcended? Surely they can, and constantly are. For language is not just constraint, it is also opportunity. The creative potential of language is hard to overemphasise. Language is a tool of thought. Rather than simply being channels of discourse, then, I want to assert the human role as an agent of discourse – at least potentially, even if this capacity is rarely fully realised. Language is a door to freedom rather than a deterministic fetter.

Bartlett's (1932: 213) early assertion of consciousness as permitting the individual to 'turn round upon its own schemata'; Kelly's (1955) emphasis on the capacity of the individual to exhibit 'constructive alternativism', and Sartre's (1958) discovery of freedom, in the same sense, as essential to consciousness, all indicate the importance (whether it is embarrassing to the scientific enterprise or not) of the self-referential nature of consciousness. Language, it would seem to me, if not the foundation of this human characteristic, certainly greatly enhances it.

The primacy of the first-person viewpoint

Postmodernism, in emphasising the way in which the person is enmeshed in their cultural and historical moment, sets aside the personal perspective, as do most of the viewpoints reviewed in this book. Yet the first-person viewpoint – the individual perspective that I myself have (it is *my* lifeworld) – must be the position from which studies of human nature in general and of psychology in particular start. We are the thing we are studying in this instance – we ourselves. Objective accounts of human nature, which assume that we are a feature of the biology or of the impersonal social world, and which describe and explain us as such, forget, as Merleau-Ponty (1962: ix) pointed out, that it is only in terms of our actual subjective lived experience of such things as identity and perception that objective accounts of these things have any meaning. Research, therefore, must begin with the first-person viewpoint on the lifeworld.

The human level versus postmodern and evolutionary purposelessness

It would seem arbitrary to both postmodern and Darwinist authors to centre on the human person as a basis of study. Both schools of thought have taken pride in having shifted research from a human focus, arguing that individuals are best understood and their actions explained when an external (biological, 'behavioural' or societal) perspective is adopted. The first-person viewpoint I have just emphasised is rejected. I am to be understood as an example of my species, or a member of my culture, or as the mere locus of interaction of a number of variables. Moreover, postmodern and Darwinian thinking teach us that the biological and the social have no 'aim'. In this sense it is right to say that, whether we are to tackle human nature from a biological or a social direction, there is no 'purpose' to be sought. The individual is a participant in neither a great chain of evolutionary progress nor a historical movement of societal improvement.

In advocating a position which is counter to these, I am not contradicting the main insights of the various schools of thought discussed in the book. I do not take the view that, on the grand scale of society or biology, there is any teleological arrow. There is no built-in directionality to human nature. On the other hand, when it comes to understanding at the level of the individual, then it is right to see choice amongst alternatives as purposeful. One line of action is chosen over another *in order to* fulfil some aim. And this requires analysis.

The lifeworld as neither exclusively subjective nor exclusively objective

The assertion of the primacy of the first-person viewpoint in understanding the human world carries with it a danger, if 'viewpoint' is regarded as *purely* subjective. As Smail (e.g. 1993) has not tired of arguing, concern with psychodynamics, the inner world and subjectivity may neglect the fact that the person's lifeworld – their actual, lived experience – is not one-sidedly subjective but has to do with the real, outer world of relationships (or loneliness), work (or unemployment) and so on. The first-person viewpoint is of the real world (from my position) – or equally it is my personal view of the (real) world. In other words neither subjectivity nor objectivity alone are appropriate; the lifeworld is a personal amalgam. It is of great importance for the correct understanding of human nature to avoid that dualism which separates the inner and the outer, and see that the personal lifeworld relates to a real context and needs to be understood with regard to that context.

It is worth mentioning here that the material circumstances of the person, which will provide one 'pole' of their lifeworld, include the social and economic facts of gender, race, and class inequality.

The subjective individuality of the person must be presupposed

Finally, I am bound by my own lived experience of personhood to assent to the Sartrean assertion of the irreducible personal existence of the individual. Whatever causal conditions – social or biological – which may in some sense have occasioned the development of personal characteristics (and the reader will have formed their own preferences amongst the viewpoints discussed here), I cannot conscientiously doubt my inner 'ownership' of that person. This does not prejudge the issue of freedom or agency. What it does do is to question the systematic forgetfulness within psychology of the 'deep subjective reality' with which it deals. Searle (1997), with his argument for the non-reducibility of consciousness, is an important ally here.

As we have seen at various points in this book, the notion of selfhood is best regarded as a construction. However, this is not the case with *one's sense of personal individuality*. The self in this latter sense is, I think (and this is a point made by William James [1890], *presupposed* in the whole of psychology. It is not deduced, derived, or discovered. If biology supplies the preconditions for selfhood, and society supplies the means by which self-reflection can occur and a specific personal identity be espoused, nevertheless, the *personal sense of being a self* cannot be assimilated to these structures and processes. The personal sense of being a self must, as I say, be presupposed by psychology, it is not open to further investigation. As Sartre put it:

> My being was that deep subjective reality which was beyond everything that could be said about it and which could not be classified. . . . What is there, in itself and before itself, is a total, profound reality, one that is in a certain manner infinite. It is the being, the person's being.
>
> (Sartre, in de Beauvoir, 1985: 242–243)

With this insight we have a statement of the limit of the analysis of human nature; an indication of the experiential basis on which psychology and related sciences are founded, and – most importantly – a suggestion of the fundamental value which should govern both theoretical and applied work in these disciplines.

Glossary

Glossary

Terms specific to particular theories are defined in the relevant chapters. Here I confine my attention to technical terminology with general application. Words in definitions which are printed in **bold** are defined elsewhere in the Glossary.

agency The capacity of the individual to actively and purposely cause effects in the world. This is denied by **determinists** for whom all actions are, in the final analysis, caused by factors outside the conscious intention of the person.

behaviourism *Methodological* behaviourism restricts investigation to observables (stimuli and associated responses) on the ground of scientific objectivity. Skinner's *radical behaviourism* makes no such stipulation, but argues that, as a matter of fact, individual behaviour is determined by 'forces in the environment'.

cognitivism An approach to the investigation of such cognitive processes as perceiving, thinking and remembering which supposes that they can be modelled in terms of the transformation of information.

constructionism Rather than thinking or acting directly by reference to, or in response to, some 'objective reality', constructionism takes the view that the individual's behaviour is the outcome of their personal construction of the situation. *Social* constructionism emphasises the role of socially available resources such as language in such constructs.

deconstruction The investigation of text, or analogies to text, which brings to light inconsistencies of many kinds such that, in the end, the meaning is shown to be indecipherable. It is supposed that all texts are, ultimately, anomalous.

determinism Thought and action is to be understood as the lawful outcome of certain factors – maybe biological, maybe social – which affect the individual. In the end the individual has no personal **agency**.

discourse analysis The study of the socially available resources which individuals employ to make sense of, and act in their world. Typically, individuals are assumed to be simply the channels of such resources rather than having any truly personal perspective.

discursive psychology The specific application of **discourse analysis** to the investigation of psychological discourse. For instance, how does one justifiably present oneself as 'doing remembering'?

dualism The **ontological** view that there are two quite distinct realms of reality, often the *mental* and the *physical.*

epistemology The philosophical search for a means of establishing the undoubted truth of the 'facts' we claim to know.

evolution The theory that species are differentiated, and either survive or become extinct, as a result of adaptedness to the environment.

evolutionary psychology The characteristics of contemporary human beings are regarded as the product of earlier evolutionary selection. Akin to **sociobiology**, but emphasising that cognitive traits ought to be seen as underlying behavioural ones.

existentialism The view that, rather than simply expressing 'human nature', individuals make choices in the very manner in which they construe their situation. Self is the pattern of such choices; the capacity to construe is freedom.

hermeneutics The clarification of the way in which meaning is embodied in a text or text-analogue. So hermeneutics is the theory of interpretation.

lifeworld The person's own experience or understanding of their situation. An amalgam of objectivity and subjectivity, it refers to the real world from the individual's perspective.

modernism The view that there is a discernible, underlying reality to which human knowledge can progressively approximate. Thus there are, in principle, firm criteria by which efforts in every field can be judged.

ontology The philosophical search for an indubitable basis for asserting in what the nature of reality consists. The conclusion of many thinkers is that reality has two modes: the mental and the physical (see **dualism**). The theory of being.

phenomenology Often, any theory which takes personal experience as basic is written of as 'phenomenological'. More properly, it is the description of the essential characteristics of the various forms of experience, and of experience as such. Ordinary experiences may be the starting point, but the eventual description greatly refines these.

positivism The **modernist** view of scientific research that assumes that there is one unified and consistent underlying reality which may be progressively uncovered and modelled. Such models are, ideally, systems of variables – causes and effects – expressible numerically.

postmodernism In contrast to **modernism**, it is not assumed that there is one unequivocal reality to which knowledge gradually approximates. Rather, a social **constructionist** view is taken of knowledge, and our understanding of the world is taken to be culturally **determined**.

psychoanalysis A theory of psychological **determinism**, which is also a **hermeneutic** theory, emphasising the unconscious causes of thought and action. The interpretation of behaviour in terms of such causes is intended and expected to have a therapeutic effect.

sociobiology The explanation of animal behaviour, including that of humans, in terms of its adaptiveness, at some stage, in the evolution of the species (see **evolutionary psychology**).

symbolic interactionism Human behaviour is primarily to be seen as the outcome of the individual's membership of the social group. Thought and action are mediated by symbols – the paramount system of which is language. Mental activity and identity are outcomes of early social experience.

teleology Any account of a process which entails purposeful direction or some goal to which the process tends. It is as if the reason for an event lies in the future. In contrast, cause-and-effect processes have the cause *precede* its effect.

Bibliography

Alcock, J. (1984) *Animal Behavior: An Evolutionary Approach* (3rd edn), Sunderland, Mass.: Sinauer.

Anderson, J.R. (1990) *Cognitive Psychology and its Implications* (3rd edn), New York: Freeman.

Armstrong, D.M. (1981) *The Nature of Mind*, Brighton: Harvester.

Ashworth, P.D. (1979) *Social Interaction and Consciousness*, Chichester: John Wiley.

Ashworth, P.D. (1985) 'L'Enfer, c'est les autres: Goffman's Sartrism', *Human Studies*, 8, 97–168.

Austin, J. (1962) *How to Do Things with Words*, Oxford: Oxford University Press.

Baddeley, A.D. (1986) *Working Memory*, Oxford: Oxford University Press.

Baddeley, A.D. (1990) *Human Memory: Theory and Practice*, Hove, UK: Lawrence Erlbaum Associates Ltd.

Baldwin, J.D. (1986) *George Herbert Mead: A Unifying Theory for Sociology*, Newbury Park, Calif.: Sage.

Bibliography

Bannister, D. and Fransella, F. (1986) *Inquiring Man: The Theory of Personal Constructs* (3rd edn), London: Routledge.

Barash, D. (1979) *Sociobiology: The Whisperings Within*, New York: Harper and Row.

Barkow, J.H., Cosmides, L. and Tooby, J. (1992) *The Adapted Mind: Evolutionary Psychology and the Generation of Culture*, New York: Oxford University Press.

Bartlett, F.C. (1932) *Remembering: A Study in Experimental and Social Psychology*, Cambridge: Cambridge University Press.

Bateman, A. and Holmes, J. (1995) *Introduction to Psychoanalysis: Contemporary Theory and Practice*, London: Routledge.

Bates, E., Benigni, L., Bretherton, I., Camaioni, L. and Volterra, V. (1979) *The Emergence of Symbols: Cognition and Communication in Infancy*, New York: Academic Press.

de Beauvoir, S. (1984) *Adieux: A Farewell to Sartre*, London: Penguin.

de Beauvoir, S. (1988) *The Second Sex*, London: Pan Books.

van den Berg, J.H. (1972) *A Different Existence: Principles of Phenomenological Psychopathology*, Pittsburgh: Duquesne University Press.

Billig, M. (1996) *Arguing and Thinking: A Rhetorical Approach to Social Psychology* (2nd edn), Cambridge: Cambridge University Press.

Blackman, D.E. (1991) 'B.F. Skinner and G.H. Mead: on biological science and social science', *Journal of the Experimental Analysis of Behavior*, 55, 251–265.

Burman, E. and Parker, I. (eds) (1993) *Discourse Analytic Research: Repertoires and Readings of Texts in Action*, London: Routledge.

Burr, V. and Butt, T. (1992) *Invitation to Personal Construct Psychology*, London: Whurr.

Caudill, W. (1962) 'Review of Goffman, *Asylums*', *American Journal of Sociology*, 68, 366–369.

Chomsky, N. (1959) 'A review of Skinner's *Verbal Behavior*', *Language*, 35, 26–58.

Craik, K.J.W. (1943) *The Nature of Explanation*, Cambridge: Cambridge University Press.

Danto, A. (1991) *Sartre* (2nd edn), London: Collins.

Darwin, C. ([1859] 1994) *The Origin of Species by Means of Natural Selection*, London: Senate.

Dawkins, R. (1976) *The Selfish Gene*, Oxford: Oxford University Press.

Dawkins, R. (1979) 'Twelve misunderstandings of kin selection', *Zeitschrift für Tiederpsychologie*, 51, 184–200.

Dawkins, R. (1982) *The Extended Phenotype*, Oxford: Oxford University Press.

Dawkins, R. (1989) *The Selfish Gene* (2nd edn), Oxford: Oxford University Press.

Derrida, J. (1976) *Of Grammatology*, Baltimore, Md.: Johns Hopkins University Press.

Derrida, J. (1978) *Writing and Difference*, London: Routledge and Kegan Paul.

Derrida, J. (1981) *Dissemination*, London: The Athlone Press.

Dobzhansky, T. (1937) *Genetics and the Origin of Species*, New York: Columbia University Press.

Eckhart (ed. O. Davies) (1994) *Meister Eckhart: Selected Writings*, London: Penguin.

Edwards, D. and Potter, J. (1992) *Discursive Psychology*, London: Sage.

Fell, J.P. (1970) 'Sartre's theory of motivation: some clarifications', *Journal of the British Society for Phenomenology*, 1 (2), 27–34.

Ferster, C.B. and Skinner, B.F. (1957) *Schedules of Reinforcement*, New York: Appleton-Century-Crofts.

Fodor, J.A. (1965) 'Could meaning be an r_m?', *Journal of Verbal Learning and Verbal Behavior*, 4, 73–81.

Foucault, M. (1971) *Madness and Civilization: A History of Insanity in the Age of Reason*, London: Tavistock.

Foucault, M. (1972) *The Archaeology of Knowledge*, London: Tavistock.

Foucault, M. (1973a) *Birth of the Clinic: An Archaeology of Medical Perception*, New York: Vintage.

Foucault, M. (1973b) *The Order of Things: An Archaeology of the Human Sciences*, New York: Vintage.

Foucault, M. (1977) *Discipline and Punish*, London: Allen Lane.

Foucault, M. (1981) *The Will to Knowledge* (The History of Sexuality, vol. 1), Harmondsworth: Penguin.

Foucault, M. (1987) *The Use of Pleasure* (The History of Sexuality, vol. 2), Harmondsworth: Penguin.

Foucault, M. (1990) *The Care of the Self* (The History of Sexuality, vol. 3), Harmondsworth: Penguin.

Freud, S. (1912) 'The dynamics of transference', in S. Freud (1957) *Standard Edition* (vol. 12), London: The Hogarth Press and The Institute of Psycho-Analysis (pp. 97–108).

Freud, S. (1974) *Introductory Lectures on Psychoanalysis* (Pelican Freud Library vol. 1), Harmondsworth: Penguin.

Freud, S. (1976) *The Interpretation of Dreams* (Pelican Freud Library vol. 4), Harmondsworth: Penguin.

Freud, S. (1977) *On Sexuality* (Pelican Freud Library vol. 7), Harmondsworth: Penguin.

Freud, S. (1979) *Case Histories II* (Pelican Freud Library vol. 9), Harmondsworth: Penguin.

Freud, S. (1984) *On Metapsychology: The Theory of Psychoanalysis* (Pelican Freud Library vol. 11), Harmondsworth: Penguin.

Freud, S. (1986) *Historical and Expository Works on Psychoanalysis* (Pelican Freud Library vol. 15), Harmondsworth: Penguin.

Gadamer, H.-G. (1975) *Truth and Method*, New York: Seabury Press.

Giddens, A. (1988) 'Goffman as a systematic social theorist', in P. Drew and A. Wootton (eds) *Erving Goffman: Exploring the Interaction Order*, Cambridge: Polity Press (pp. 250–279).

Gillin, C.T. (1975) 'Freedom and the limits of social behaviourism: a comparison of selected themes from the works of G.H. Mead and Martin Buber', *Sociology*, 9, 24–47.

Giorgi, A.P. (1970) *Psychology as a Human Science: A Phenomenologically-Based Account*, New York: Harper and Row.

Goffman, E. (1968a) *Asylums: Essays on the Social Situation of Mental Patients and Other Inmates*, Harmondsworth: Penguin.

Goffman, E. (1968b) *Stigma: Notes on the Management of Spoiled Identity*, Harmondsworth: Penguin.

Goffman, E. (1971) *The Presentation of Self in Everyday Life*, Harmondsworth: Penguin.

Goffman, E. (1972a) *Encounters: Two Studies in the Sociology of Interaction*, Harmondsworth: Penguin.

Goffman, E. (1972b) *Interaction Ritual: Essays on Face-to-Face Behaviour*, Harmondsworth: Penguin.

Goffman, E. (1972c) *Strategic Interaction*, Oxford: Blackwell.

Goffman, E. (1972d) *Relations in Public*, Harmondsworth: Penguin.

Goffman, E. (1974) *Frame Analysis: An Essay on the Organization of Experience*, New York: Harper and Row.

Goffman, E. (1983) 'The interaction order', *American Sociological Review*, 48, 1–17.

Gonos, G. (1977) '"Situation" versus "frame": The "interactionist" and the "structuralist" analyses of everyday life', *American Sociological Review*, 42, 854–867.

Gould, S.J. (1977) 'Caring groups and selfish genes', *Natural History*, 86 (12), 20–24.

Gould, S.J. (1997) 'Darwinian fundamentalism', *The New York Review of Books*, 12 June, 34–37.

Habermas, J. (1987) *The Philosophical Discourse of Modernity*, Cambridge: Polity Press.

Hamilton, W.D. (1972) 'Altruism and related phenomena, mainly in social insects', *Annual Review of Ecology and Systematics*, 3, 193–232.

Hampson, P.J. and Morris, P.E. (1996) *Understanding Cognition*, Oxford: Blackwell.

Harré, R. (ed.) (1976) *Life Sentences: Aspects of the Social Role of Language*, Chichester: John Wiley.

Harré, R. (ed.) (1977) *Personality*, Oxford: Blackwell.

Harré, R. (1979) *Social Being: A Theory for Social Psychology*, Oxford: Blackwell.

Harré, R. (1983) *Personal Being: A Theory for Individual Psychology*, Oxford: Blackwell.

Harré, R. (1991) *Physical Being: A Theory for a Corporeal Psychology*, Oxford: Blackwell.

Harré, R. (1998) *The Singular Self*, London: Sage.

Harré, R. and Gillett, G. (1994) *The Discursive Mind*, London: Sage.

Harré, R. and Secord, P.F. (1972) *The Explanation of Social Behaviour*, Oxford: Blackwell.

Harré, R. and Stearns, P. (1995) *Discursive Psychology in Practice*, London: Sage.

Heidegger, M. (1962) *Being and Time*, Oxford: Blackwell.

Heider, F. (1958) *The Psychology of Interpersonal Relations*, New York: John Wiley.

Hollway, W. (1989) *Subjectivity and Method in Psychology: Gender, Meaning and Science*, London: Sage.

Husserl, E. (1970) *The Crisis of European Sciences and Transcendental Phenomenology*, Evanston, Ill.: Northwestern University Press.

James, W. (1890) *The Principles of Psychology* (2 vols), New York: Holt.

Jones, E. (eds L. Trilling and S. Marcus) (1964) *The Life and Work of Sigmund Freud*, London: Penguin.

Kelly, G.A. (1955) *The Psychology of Personal Constructs* (2 vols), New York: Norton [reprinted 1991, London: Routledge].

Kuhn, T.S. (1970) *The Structure of Scientific Revolutions* (2nd edn), Chicago: Chicago University Press.

Kvale, S. (ed.) (1992) *Psychology and Postmodernism*, London: Sage.

Kvale, S. and Grenness, C.E. (1967) 'Skinner and Sartre: towards a radical phenomenology of behaviour?', *Review of Existential Psychology and Psychiatry*, 7, 128–148.

Lindsay, P.H. and Norman, D.A. (1972) *Human Information Processing: An Introduction to Psychology*, New York: Academic Press.

Logie, R.H. (1995) *Visuo-Spatial Working Memory*, Hove, UK: Lawrence Erlbaum Associates Ltd.

Luijpen, W.A. (1966) *Phenomenology and Humanism*, Pittsburgh: Duquesne University Press.

Lyotard, J.-F. (1984) *The Postmodern Condition: A Report on Knowledge*, Minneapolis: University of Minnesota Press.

Maher, B.A. (1969) *Clinical Psychology and Personality: The Collected Papers of George Kelly*, Huntington, N.Y.: Wiley.

Manis, J.G. and Meltzer, B.N. (eds) (1972) *Symbolic Interaction: A Reader in Social Biology* (2nd edn), Boston: Allyn and Bacon.

Mead, G.H. (1934) *Mind, Self and Society*, Chicago: Chicago University Press.

Meltzer, B.N. (1972) 'Mead's social psychology', in J.G. Manis and B.N. Meltzer (eds) *Symbolic Interaction* (2nd edn), Boston: Allyn and Bacon (pp. 4–22).

Merleau-Ponty, M. (1962) *Phenomenology of Perception*, London: Routledge and Kegan Paul.

Merquior, J.G. (1985) *Foucault*, London: Fontana.

Miller, G.A., Gallanter, E. and Pribram, K.H. (1960) *Plans and the Structure of Behavior*, New York: Holt, Rinehart and Winston.

Mills, C.W. (1940) 'Situated actions and vocabularies of motive', *American Sociological Review*, 5, 904–913.

Mowrer, O. (1960) *Learning Theory and the Symbolic Processes*, New York: Wiley.

Murdoch, I. (1967) *Sartre*, London: Collins.

Naegele, K.D. (1956) 'Review of Goffman, *The Presentation of Self in Everyday Life*', *American Sociological Review*, 21, 631–632.

Neisser, U. (1967) *Cognitive Psychology*, New York: Appleton-Century-Crofts.

Newell, A., Shaw, J. and Simon, H. (1961) 'Computer simulation of human thinking', *Science*, 134, 2011–2017.

Norris, C. (1987) *Derrida*, London: Fontana.

Palmer, R.E. (1969) *Hermeneutics: Interpretation Theory in Schleiermacher, Dilthey, Heidegger, and Gadamer*, Evanston, Ill.: Northwestern University Press.

Piaget, J. (1977) *The Origin of Intelligence in the Child*, Harmondsworth: Penguin.

Popper, K. (1959) *The Logic of Scientific Discovery*, New York: Harper and Row.

Potter, J. and Wetherell, M. (1987) *Discourse and Social Psychology: Beyond Attitudes and Behaviour*, London: Sage.

Potter, J. and Wetherell, M. (1995) 'Discourse analysis', in J. Smith, R. Harré and L. van Langenhove (eds) *Rethinking Methods in Psychology*, London: Sage (pp. 80–92).

Richards, G. (1996) *Putting Psychology in its Place: An Introduction from a Critical Historical Perspective*, London: Routledge.

Richelle, M.N. (1993) *B.F. Skinner: A Reappraisal*, Hove, UK: Lawrence Erlbaum Associates Ltd.

Ricoeur, P. (1970) *Freud and Philosophy: An Essay on Interpretation*, New Haven, Conn.: Yale University Press.

Ricoeur, P. (1971) 'The model of the text: meaningful action considered as text', *Social Research*, 38, 527–562.

Ricoeur, P. (1998) *Critique and Conviction*, Cambridge: Polity Press.

Rogers, C.R. (1967) *On Becoming a Person: A Therapist's View of Psychotherapy*, London: Constable.

Rosch, E. and Lloyd, B.B. (eds) (1978) *Cognition and Categorisation*, Hillsdale, N.J.: Lawrence Erlbaum Associates Inc.

Sahlins, M. (1977) *The Use and Abuse of Biology: An Anthropological Critique of Sociobiology*, London: Tavistock.

Sartre, J.-P. (1946) *In Camera*, London: Hamish Hamilton.

Sartre, J.-P. (1949) *Baudelaire*, London: Horizon Press.

Sartre, J.-P. (1957) *The Transcendence of the ego*, New York: Farrar, Straus and Giroux.

Sartre, J.-P. (1958) *Being and Nothingness*, New York: Philosophical Library.

Sartre, J.-P. (1962) *Sketch for a Theory of the Emotions*, London: Methuen.

Sartre, J.-P. (1965) *Nausea*, London: Penguin.

Sartre, J.-P. (1972) *The Psychology of Imagination*, London: Methuen.

Schafer, R. (1983) *The Analytic Attitude*, London: The Hogarth Press and The Institute of Psycho-Analysis.

Scheler, M. (1954) *The Nature of Sympathy*, London: Routledge and Kegan Paul.

Schilpp, P.A. (1981) *The Philosophy of Jean-Paul Sartre*, La Salle, Ill.: Open Court.

Searle, J.R. (1997) *The Mystery of Consciousness*, London: Granta.

Skinner, B.F. (1953) *Science and Human Behaviour*, New York: The Free Press.

Skinner, B.F. (1957) *Verbal Behavior*, New York: Appleton-Century-Crofts.

Skinner, B.F. (1964) 'Behaviorism at fifty', in T.W. Wann, (ed.) *Behaviorism and Phenomenology: Contrasting Bases for Modern Psychology*, Chicago: Chicago University Press (pp. 79–108).

Skinner, B.F. (1971) *Beyond Freedom and Dignity*, New York: Knopf.

Skinner, B.F. (1978) *Reflections on Behaviorism and Society*, Englewood Cliffs, N.J.: Prentice-Hall.

Skinner, B.F. (1980) *Notebooks*, Englewood Cliffs, N.J.: Prentice-Hall.

Skinner, B.F. (1993) *About Behaviourism*, London: Penguin.

Slater, A. and Bremner, G. (eds) (1989) *Infant Development*, Hove, UK: Lawrence Erlbaum Associates Ltd.

Smail, D. (1993) *The Origins of Unhappiness: A New Understanding of Personal Distress*, London: HarperCollins.

Smith, J., Harré, R. and van Langenhove, L. (eds) (1995) *Rethinking Methods in Psychology*, London: Sage.

Stearns, P. (1995) 'Emotion', in R. Harré and P. Stearns (eds) *Discursive Psychology in Practice*, London: Sage.

Tooby, J. and Cosmides, L. (1992) 'The psychological foundations of culture', in J.H. Barkow, L. Cosmides and J. Tooby, *The Adapted Mind: Evolutionary Psychology and the Generation of Culture*, New York: Oxford University Press (pp. 19–136).

Trivers, R.L. (1971) 'The evolution of reciprocal altruism', *Quarterly Review of Biology*, 46, 35–57.

Tulving, E. (1983) *Elements of Episodic Memory*, Oxford: Oxford University Press.

Turkheimer, E. (1998) 'Heritability and biological explanation', *Psychological Review*, 105, 782–791.

Valentine, E. (1992) *Conceptual Issues in Psychology* (2nd edn), London: Routledge.

Ward, K. (1998) *Religion and Human Nature*, Oxford: Oxford University Press.

Weinsheimer, J.C. (1985) *Gadamer's Hermeneutics: A Reading of 'Truth and Method'*, New Haven, Conn.: Yale University Press.

Weiskrantz, L. (1988) 'Some contributions of neuropsychology of vision and memory to the problem of consciousness', in A.J. Marcel and

E. Bisiach (eds) *Consciousness in Contemporary Science*, New York: Oxford University Press (pp. 183–199).
Welford, A.T. (1968) *Fundamentals of Skill*, London: Methuen.
Wider, K.V. (1997) *The Bodily Nature of Consciousness*, New York: Cornell University Press.
Wilson, E.O. (1975) *Sociobiology: The New Synthesis*, Cambridge, Mass.: Harvard University Press.
Wilson, E.O. (1978) *On Human Nature*, Cambridge, Mass.: Harvard University Press.
Wilson, E.O. (1996) *In Search of Nature*, London: Penguin.
Wynne-Edwards, V.C. (1962) *Animal Dispersion in Relation to Social Behaviour*, New York: Hafner.

Index